Why Our Children Will Be Atheists

Why Our Children Will Be Atheists

*The Last 100 Years of Religion, and
the Dawn of a World without Gods*

Albert Williams

First Edition

ISBN 978-0-620-58801-0 (print)

ISBN 978-0-620-58802-7 (ebook)

Printed in the United States of America

"And he came to a stream in his journey, and he knew the world was about to change as he crossed it. In front of him was a vast land full of gods. He knew he had to go there, to face them all. But as he crossed the stream into the unknown, he realized the gods were all a delusion. He had no fear; but as he looked back, he realized that it was not the gods themselves who might kill him, but those who believed in the delusion of the gods. He also knew that he might never see the end of his journey, but that soon others would cross the stream, and the unknown would become the known and the unthinkable the norm.

"And as he felt the sun and wind on his skin and the cosmos all around him, he did not regret."

Table of Contents

Foreword

The knife cuts deep into the body of the young girl, and she squirms as she is pinned down by two strong adults, her screams muffled by the cloth pushed far back into her mouth. Her attackers are untouched by her pain and suffering; a trance comes over them as they proceed to viciously and savagely harvest her body parts. Body parts intended for the gods.

The priest looks down at his audience with contentment; the atmosphere is electric and laden with power. Tonight he is the tool of God, bringing God's word to the people. God will be satisfied with his work and message: a message of obedience to God, to find his mercy and salvation. Pity those believing in other Gods, for God's curse awaits them in the afterlife.

By now the square has filled with people, people with no hope, people for whom a season of drought has brought misery and poverty and hunger. A day of prayer has been called; a day to call on God to open the heavens; a day to ask for forgiveness for whatever it was they did to displease Him, to beg Him to be merciful. A prayer for the rain to begin, to alleviate the drought-stricken country.

The scientist pushes back his chair; the dating report for the fossil in front of him is just in, putting the age of these early human remains at several million years. They were found in the Great Rift Valley of eastern Africa, a place many have come to regard as the birthplace of humankind. The television across the room broadcasts the first images of the latest space shuttle returning to Earth, from a mission that gathered space dust that will be soon be dated at more than 4.6 *billion* years old.

·

In this book, the author reveals the origins of our gods, in particular where and how they became our gods. He discusses the profound impact of these gods on our lives, and the measures taken by their followers to keep those gods alive. The story of the Earth and the origins of life then take the forefront, after which the last 100 years of religion is predicted, and the reasons why this will be the case. The new era is anticipated by many: a post-God era in which the human race will emerge from its religious past with a new understanding of the universe and humanity—a new model with which to face the next few thousand years on Earth and elsewhere. It is a book that predicts the end of religion as we know it. The transformation has started.

CHAPTER 1

The Birth of Religion

The End of Religion in the Next 100 Years

Humanity is entering the final century of religion as we know it: the conclusion of an era that has lasted literally millions of years, spanning our origins from primitive hominid to the discovery of evolution and the true origins of life.

The history of humankind is to split in two, a bygone era of ignorance and religion and a new era of knowledge and reason.

The next century represents the transitional period between these epochs of thought. By the end of this period, Judaism, Christianity, Islam, Hinduism, and so many other faiths will fade and, ultimately, disappear. The last living generation of believers will be replaced by new generations for whom religion will be a faint memory.

Will the gods still exist at all by 2120? Or will one of our current Gods finally manifest itself once and for all to obliterate all the other religions and gods, merging the supernatural and human worlds at last.

The world is about to change and three outcomes are possible:

1. Religion will cease to exist, having been replaced by a new model of human behavior and understanding;
2. Religion as we know it will change to adapt to a modern world; or
3. Religious ideology will replace our current knowledge, transforming the world into a backward theocracy.

Why Our Children Will be Atheists fearlessly examines our current major religions, their origins, and the path of their final demise. This book also lays bare the origins of the current gods, from Allah to Jehovah to Shiva and all the rest, whether monotheistic or pantheonic. It begins by examining the evidence we've uncovered regarding primitive religions—evidence dominated by myth, ritual, taboo, and superstition— and shows how so much of each is still present in our current religions.

As the global human population increased from a few thousand to tens and hundreds of thousands, and then into the millions, humanity entered an inevitable transformation from hunter-gatherers to agriculturists—inevitable because it was the only way to support large numbers of people. This transformation also triggered the evolution of primitive belief systems into the more complex ones we know today. As nomadic groups first concentrated around abundant resources and then learned to control them, our first major gods were born: the early deities of Ur and Sumer; later, the more sophisticated gods, from Hindu to Egyptian to Judaism, Christianity and other.

The book then asks if today's gods were *really* always there, presiding over the world since its creation, each the ultimate Creator and Ruler of our cosmos—or if, in fact, they ever really existed?

The author traces the religions of our current society, from their origins 10,000+ years ago as basic ritual and superstition, on through the development of full priesthoods and religious orders. The human race's powerful dependence and reliance upon religion is then considered in detail. He describes the ordeal of a boy, trapped by a deadly sickness, using his god and religion to find answers. He also explores the psychological impact of religion on human thought and behavior throughout history.

Next, *Why Our Children Will be Atheists* tackles the question of whether religion imbues a person with better morals and essential goodness. In particular, it critically discusses research claiming that religious children are happier and more content than their non-religious counterparts. Also examined are the powerful mechanisms that religion deploys to ensure its survival, and the use of the state to advance religion.

The final section part of the book briefly outlines our current knowledge of the universe, the origins of life, and its evolution, all of which are gradually replacing our notions of Special Creation. The new, emergent phase of human spirituality is then described, representing a model that will eventually render current faiths irrelevant, heralding the beginning of a religion-free era.

The Different Modern Religions

The modern world is witness to a wide variety of belief systems and religions. Most of these religions group into geographical regions, as a result of military conquests by specific religious factions. About two billion modern people profess belief in the Judeo-Christian God; 1.6 billion identify as Muslims, believing in Allah; and about one billion others are grouped as Hindu, worshipping a number of gods in a large pantheon. Some 400-1,000 million people adhere to Buddhism, while roughly one billion people believe in more traditional religions. We also have a billion people subscribing to the Chinese beliefs of Taoism and Confucianism. The world is abounding with different gods, with nearly all their followers claiming theirs to be the true and only God. So which one really is?

To find the answers, we need to delve into the past. If we backtrack beyond the modern history of humankind, we find that many gods have disappeared in the relatively recent past. The great Egyptian god Ra, the Sun God who was once among the most powerful in the world, is no longer worshipped to any appreciable extent. For all intents and purposes, Ra is dead. The same goes for the omnipotent Greek Thunder God, Zeus, and his Roman avatar Jupiter. Our history is littered with the corpses of gods.

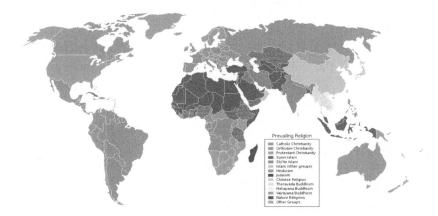

Figure 1: Religions practiced by the majority of religious persons in the world (excluding non-religious), closely mirroring military conquests in the past

As we have progressed technologically over the ages, we have brought our gods with us. The knowledge passed from one generation to the next has typically included our understanding and worship of said gods. But is there still a place for such gods in a world where human beings are free to express doubt and to otherwise question and research religion on their own? Will our current gods still exist 100 years from today, or will they disappear from our collective consciousness?

Or will one God finally manifest and speak out once and for all, relying no more on pure faith for His or Her power?

Many of us are mystified by the silence of our gods. They refuse to speak or appear to us, apart from unconfirmed reports which may be delusions caused by emotional stress or other factors. So why are we nonetheless willing to murder others in the name of religion, even those who worship the same gods slightly differently? Why is our religion not revealed to each of us directly by our god? Why instead is it forced on us, based upon our birthplaces and parental origin?

A child born in North America will probably take the Judeo-Christian God as the one and only god, while a child born in Saudi Arabia will probably take His Islamic counterpart, Allah, as the one true god. Both gods stem from the same roots and are, in fact, aspects of the very same god; yet we are notoriously willing to kill each other to defend our visions of these gods, who as omnipotent, omniscient, omnipresent beings should certainly require no such defense.

Do we *require* a god or gods to explain life and death and the mighty universe surrounding us? How do we explain this remarkable planet of ours? We *need* answers to these vast questions, and most religions exist to feed the psychological functions driving this need. Ancient interpretations of the world depended on our limited knowledge of the universe to explain our purpose for existing, and the purpose of the universe around us. Our knowledge is much less limited now; yet we cling to spiritual explanations that are thousands of years out of date.

Our inevitable deaths, and the deaths of our loved ones, act as primary motivators for the survival of our gods, because the religions built around them provide consolation and answer the eternal *Why?* that humans shout at the world. Our own sense of self-worth refuses to accept that our existence is a wonderful accident, and that there is no true purpose in it, except for the purposes we make for ourselves.

In this book, we'll boldly confront, examine, and dissect our gods down to their origins, and attempt to explain how the psychological composition of humans makes giving up our gods so difficult. Once done with that, we'll attempt to envision a world without our current gods. While those steeped in religion would naturally expect a dark, cold world with evil or, at least, disinterest reigning supreme, the truth is that this new world will be one of understanding, tolerance, and mutual respect—and will represent the true beginning of our search for purpose and meaning in the universe.

Once we've struck out on this new bright path, the era of gods and religion will quickly fade to an historical footnote, just one step in the *true* spiritual journey of humankind.

Where did our First Gods come from

Where did our first gods come from? Can we find any evidence of them, or their respective religions, in the beginnings of humankind? If so, perhaps learning about and trying to understand our ancient gods or religions might provide some clues to our modern gods. Were today's Abrahamic, Hindu, Native American, or African tribal gods already present in those ancient times? Were they only observing our ancient ancestors for long millennia? If so, why did they wait until just a few thousand years ago, at best, to make themselves known to humanity, demanding worship as the only true gods?

Unfortunately, our knowledge regarding the very first religions practiced by human beings is scarce; time has erased most of the evidence, especially once we pass beyond written history. Did those first human genuses such as the Australopithecines of Olduvai Gorge believe in gods? Were the flowers that some Neanderthals apparently buried with their dead (as evidenced by their pollen) associated with religious ritual? Our only guides are those things that endure: fertility figurines, the time-ravaged remains of human settlements, or the recording of events painted on or pecked into stone or cave walls.

No doubt many of the religious traditions people still follow today were transmitted orally for centuries, or even longer, before they were inscribed into monuments, temples, and shrines, before the first clay tablets took their cuneiform impressions or people left the evidence in the graves we open. Perhaps all these things can help us push our understanding of religion back farther than the 5,000 years or so we can interpret thus far. But we want to go back even further. Archaeological and paleontological evidence suggests that anatomically modern humans have been around for 160,000 years or more. Predecessor species of hominids go back more than 4,000,000 years. All had comparatively large brains, walked on two feet, and used their hands to make tools.

That being the case, did they use their brains to invent gods? What *did* these people believe in? Were our current gods—e.g., the Judeo-Christian God or the Muslim Allah, among many—already extant then in some form, and if they were, how can we find clues that might help us answer these questions?

Our only clues lie in the tenuous remains that archaeologists unearth from the pages of our world's geological history.

Searching for Evidence of Gods in Prehistory

Let's travel back to the period of 2.5 million-120,000 years ago, a rather lengthy stretch in which humanity gradually transitioned from our primitive origins to essentially the civilization-building, world-dominating species we are today. Until about 120,000 years ago, much of the Earth was innocent of humanity, with very small, scattered populations in the Old World that probably totaled to just a few thousand.

The only evidence we have of these people's existence consists of the few fossilized bones that were able to survive the passage of time, and the more durable stone tools they made. What they believed in or thought about didn't fossilize or otherwise freeze in time, with the exception of those tools, which were almost certainly used for hunting animals and for gathering wild plant foods. We do know from our findings that the earliest stone tool users belonged not only to a different species from today's humans, but to a different genus: *Australopithecus*, who translates as "southern ape-man." Their very simple stone tools can be found on the banks of rivers, as well as in the open spaces and caves of the deep East African rift valley where the African tectonic plate is slowly splitting into two smaller tectonic plates.

Many other sites have been discovered in Africa and elsewhere, documenting the existence of later species of these early human ancestors— and, eventually, modern humans. For example, several hundred thousand years ago, a community existed for thousands of years on the banks of the Somme River in France at Saint-Acheul. The people who lived there left behind an abundance of flint artifacts, hammer stones, and other small implements.

What were the beliefs and gods of these ancient people?

Without a time machine, it's impossible to say. People were thin on the ground back then, and the immense scale of time has erased most evidence of their existence. The Earth is too dynamic for anything to last long; preservation tends to occur only by geological accident, so we're lucky to have the evidence we do have. Nearly all their old dwellings have long since vanished, along with most of their art...if, indeed, art existed before about 20,000 years ago. This leaves us with no valid ways to draw conclusions about the thoughts or beliefs of our ancient ancestors.

However, we do know that they were making tools, and most had family structures with social order. They would have been conscious of the world they were living in, and the passage of time. Graves and other ceremonial interments are a relatively recent invention. Did the earliest humans just leave their dead behind, as animals do, or did they mourn the passing of a loved one? Where burial or cremation did occur, was it accompanied by ritual? In many cases, especially from the early days of the practice, it's impossible to tell. We have sketchy evidence and few clues. We've mentioned the flower pollen in some Neanderthal graves, suggesting that they at least buried their dead with flowers; the graves of anatomically modern humans often contain pots, chipped stone tools, and the remains of woven or braided textiles. Were these efforts to appease the gods, provide for the dead in the afterlife, or simple emblems of respect? We can only speculate at this stage. Even today, some cultures are deeply afraid of death, and are loathe to touch a dead body or use the belongings of the dead person.

In the ancient days, did people fear that the life or soul that had left a dead person might come back to harm them? Did they show respect and make offerings to appease the dead? Were they in awe of a thunderstorm's roar and its lightning dancing across the landscape, or of the moon rising in the evening, or of an earthquake shaking the ground? Did they perform the predefined actions of a ritual before a hunt, to maximize their chances of success, or after a successful hunt? Again, it's hard to say, with the erasure of most evidence across the passage of time. With luck we may make new archaeological discoveries that will offer some clues; but otherwise, most of that earlier world remains lost to us. We're better served shifting our attention to more recent times: to the period after about 30,000 years ago, when more clues become available.

Caves offered shelter and protection for our ancestors, both from the elements and more dangerous animals. By then, fire had long since been discovered. Visualize a small group of humans occupying a cave.

As night approached, the occupants would have gathered around the fire. In the most ancient of days, this would have been an eternal fire, always kept alive after the great fortune of borrowing or buying a live ember from another group, or encountering a natural wildfire. Later, people figured out how to kindle fires directly. The cries and noises of children and a few babies would have filled the cave. Outside, the evening noises of wild animals might be audible. A few hunters might recount a hunt experience they'd had that day, with, perhaps, some of them nursing wounds they had sustained. As always, there was the close presence of death and the fear that came with it.

Within such an environment, the human mind would have been aroused in an attempt to understand the world around them. Within these caves we find our first evidence of ritual belief, disclosed in drawings made on the caves walls. Some of the most striking examples occur in a cave discovered in Lascaux, France. In September 1940, teenagers Marcel Ravidat, Jacques Marsal, Georges Agnel, and Simon Coencas went for a walk in the countryside with Ravidat's dog, Robot. During their walk, they stumbled upon a hole in the ground opened up by a fallen tree. Being boys, they expanded the hole further and entered the cave they found—the first people to do so in 17,000 years. Once their eyes became accustomed to the dark, they bore witness to one of the most spectacular galleries of drawings made by prehistoric humans, as long ago as 30,000 years before present (B.P.).

Since that discovery the cave has been meticulously studied, and some scientists have concluded that the drawings offer a glimpse into the religious beliefs of these long-forgotten people. Apparently, the cave was used as a sanctuary for religious and initiation rites, as indicated by the presence of ceremonial artifacts. The evidence suggests that the cave was only visited for short times for ritualistic reasons, given that the footprints preserved in the soil mostly belonged to adults. The drawings sketched here depict mostly animals, though in one drawing a man with a bird head is shown—illustrating the role that animals played in this early religion, a religion that most probably consisted of an animistic mix of myth, ritual, and communication with the natural world.

More evidence of early religion is found in the burial practices of the dead. On 17 September 1909, Louis Capitan and Denis Peyrony discovered human remains in the La Ferrassie rockshelter near the village of Les Eyzies in the Dordogne Valley of France. The site yielded skeletal material of seven individual Neanderthals, including adults, children, infants, and fetuses, all dating from about 50,000 years ago. The adult male had been laid to rest with his arms and leg drawn close to his body; the female was tightly flexed, with her legs folded into her body, one arm against her chest. The children were found in a pit. It's clear that all five were intentionally buried at the shelter. We will probably never know what happened to this people, but there's no doubt they were buried in an organized and systematic way, hauntingly similar to the religious rituals observed by later cultures.

What stirred these primitive spiritual expressions? Already set apart from all other animals by their large brains and tool use, this ancient human species surely had the ability to analyze, remember, and reason—cultural abilities they used successfully to develop their tools, build shelters, and harness fire. That being the case, few occasions would have had more of an impact than the birth of a child after a man and woman came together, or the passing away of another person with only the empty body left behind. Add to this the unexplained (and then unexplainable) "magic" of nature, with the sun rising in the morning and crossing the sky; onset of night, and the moon following the sun's path; thunder stalking across the night sky, or the land. Fire, the turning of the leaves in the fall, snow, and so much more must have made a deep impact on the psyches of these early humans.

The grief of having a child or other loved one pass away would have stirred our ancestors to seek reasons, or at least an explanation—and to wonder if the dead person were still present, whether here or in another world. It is not surprising, then, that these human groups first set foot on the path of religion; it was a way to explain the world. It was, and remains, a way for people to reconcile the irreconcilable and keep existing themselves, a way to find solace in the uncertainty of a world filled with death. The power of music, of dancing around a fire and witnessing blood flowing from a dying animal, may also have stimulated and contributed to the religious history of humanity.

We find additional clues to the beliefs and practices of these ancient peoples in today's isolated pockets of humanity, otherwise cut off from the rest of the world and the contamination of modern religions. These peoples were much more common historically, but a few such groups survive today. The Aborigines in Australia, for example, were far removed and isolated from today's religions until well into the 18th century. We still find occasional tribes in South America and Africa that practice their age-old religions. On an island close to India we find a small population, the Sentinelese, who remain so isolated they live very much as they did 40,000 years ago—a window that lets us peek into the world of our ancient religions, and thus the origins of our gods.

Needless to say, the prevalence of such groups is rapidly diminishing as they're exposed to the modern world and absorbed into the global village. But still, we have a wealth of information from the pioneers who recorded the practices of these groups, in addition to the ongoing studies of societies. These can help us better understand our first human religions, and most importantly, enable us to identify the remnants of these ideas and beliefs in modern religions.

The Stirring of First Religions: Myths

In these ancient communities, writing had not yet been invented, and so oral storytelling was used to record and explain the natural world. These stories were told over and over again, with the storyteller always ready to embellish them with just a little more color and imagination in order to entice his audience. Even stories that began as factual eventually evolved into myths.

Many of these myths explained natural phenomena, such as storms or the rising and setting of the sun or moon. Even more importantly, many explained the origins of the world, the creation of humanity, death, and the possibility of life after death. So pervasive and powerful are such myths that many are taken as purely factual, right up to this very day; indeed, such myths have become the main friction points between science and the religious faithful.

Doubtless, most of the first religions existed of collections of myths, since anything unexplainable by direct observation still had to have an explanation. The Australian Aborigines had a myth that the rivers and lakes in Australia had been made by an enormous frog. After a long drought, all the animals came together and discovered that the frog had swallowed all the water. After many tries, an eel got the frog to laugh, and the water came gushing out to form the lakes and rivers. Other myths abounded to describe how the sun, moon, world, and stars were created.

The San people of Southern Africa had a myth that many years ago, all people and animals lived in harmony together underneath the earth, with a great master and lord of life, Kaang. Kaang then planned how he would go about rising to the upper world. One day he planted a tree with branches stretching over the whole country. He then made a hole, and led the first man up; and soon all the other people and animals followed. Kaang gathered all of them and told them to live together peacefully. He also told the humans not to make any fire, or a great evil would come over them. With nightfall, though, it became dark and cold; and one man suggested making a fire for warmth and light. Forgetting their instructions, a fire was made that scared the animals away, resulting in an unending clash between humans and animals. Fear has replaced the original friendship.

Mythology is a chief component of all religions, including today's. The Jewish, Christian and Islamic religions all include the story of Adam and Eve. On the seventh day of Creation, God planted a Garden for Man, in the center of which was the Tree of Life—the tree of the knowledge of good and evil. Adam was told not to eat any fruits from this tree; but soon Adam got lonely, and God promised him a companion. When the man fell asleep God took a rib from him and created a woman, Eve.

In the garden there lived a snake that convinced the woman to eat some of the forbidden fruit; which she did, before she gave some of the fruit to Adam. Once the fruit was eaten they realized their nakedness, and covered themselves. When God discovered this, He was angry. The snake was cursed to spending the rest of his life as a crawling animal to be hunted by man; and his descendants were cursed with the same fate. Eve and all her female ancestors were punished with painful childbirth, and by being forced to live as secondary citizens to men. Both Man and Woman were banished from the Garden forever.

There are several creation myths in Hinduism. According to one,

Before this time began, there was no Heaven, no Earth, and no space between. A vast, dark ocean washed upon the shores of nothingness and licked the edges of the night. A giant cobra floated on the waters. Asleep within its endless coils lay the Lord Vishnu. He was watched over by the mighty serpent. Everything was so peaceful and silent that Vishnu slept undisturbed by dreams or motion. From the depths, a humming sound began to tremble. It grew and spread, filling the emptiness and throbbing with energy. The night had ended. Vishnu awoke. As the dawn began to break, from Vishnu's navel grew a magnificent lotus flower. In the middle of the blossom sat Vishnu's servant, Brahma. He awaited the Lord's command. Vishnu spoke to his servant: "It is time to begin." Brahma bowed. Vishnu commanded: "Create the world."

Then Brahma split the lotus flower into three. He stretched one part into the Heavens. He made another part into the Earth. With the third part of the flower, he created the skies.

A myth presents itself as a true and factual event regardless of how irrational it may be, or how irreconcilable with experience or science. Myths also play the role of providing a moral message or example for living one's life and guiding one's behavior. While one can easily identify and recognize a myth from another religion or society, it's much more difficult (and sometimes impossible) to identify the myths of one's society or religion. Recognition of a myth normally only happens when one does not believe in the authority of the myth; e.g., a Jew believing that Christ was not the foretold Messiah, or the non-Muslim's belief that Muhammad was not, in fact, a prophet.

Some modern myths have become powerful enough to hold entire nations or groups of nations together, and serve as integral parts of their collective consciousnesses. For example, most Western nations believe fiercely in capitalism; that may be seen as an outgrowth of the myth that this form of market economy is superior to all others. That may be true or false; but whatever the case, it is so entrenched in Western society that any argument against it is sometimes perceived as unpatriotic or dangerous, even to the point of overturning the fortunes and well-beings of these nations.

In religious terms, the most influential myths are those that build on the concepts of powerful beings, myths that evolve over time to turn those beings into omnipotent deities, who rule either over one province of nature or over them all. Many ancient groups perceived the sky as sacred, a world different from the one in which we find ourselves. In such belief systems, the sky is a realm where we can soar free, like birds and insects, released from our worldly sufferings; and so most religions identify the sky with their gods, or place the gods' abode somewhere in or beyond the sky.

More profound, perhaps, are the myths based on natural phenomena that ancient people held in awe: for example, the sun. Many myths have arisen with the sun as their central motif, building until the sun emerges as or is closely associated with a god: e.g. Ancient Egypt's Ra, or the Roman Apollo. Similarly, thunder gradually evolved from a fearsome natural phenomenon into a supernatural one, associated with a god hemmed in by his own myths: Thor in Norse mythology, Shango in Yoruba/Santeria, the Thunderbirds in some Native American cultures. Generally, such gods have (mostly) human characteristics writ large; so if you sin, then the god will become angry enough to destroy or punish you.

Ancient humans also realized that time stretched out apparently eternally, at least compared to their own limited life spans. They witnessed the rise and setting of the sun, seasons passing, and people being born and dying; eventually, most individuals (now as then) realized that after death, the world would continue on without them. But why shouldn't there be eternal life? Perhaps there is, if we can just access it. This longing to become part of the world again, rather than vanish into nothingness, gave rise to all the varied beliefs in the afterlife.

Expectations about the end of the world also developed into myths found in many religions and cults. Most Judeo-Christian sects believe that there will someday be an Armageddon—a final, apocalyptic battle between Good and Evil. The historic Pawnee Indians believed that there would come a time when the world would disappear. Fierce storms and fire would come from the sky, the moon would turn red, the sun would no longer shine, and the stars would fall from Heaven.

Ritual

Also common to all these ancient religions, as well as today's, is the use of ritual. Ritual is defined as a repetitive set of actions; e.g., a rainmaker performing some action intended to induce rain. If we go to the animal world, we also find some evidence of ritual. Before embarking on a hunt, wolves come together and howl in unison with their tails raised. This conditions them to function in a pack. Our hunter ancestors practiced similar behavior. It may have started as simply as banging some stones together before starting a hunt, later evolving to include some war-like cries, stepping in a specific pattern, singing, and more. When the hunt was successful, the hunters concluded that the pre-hunt ritual had been performed successfully; if not, then clearly they had performed the ritual wrong, or without sufficient devotion.

We now have ample evidence of how ritual develops in a society, then later evolves into religion. Let's take a look at a well-excavated site in Oaxaca, Mexico, dating back 10,000 years, and follow a small group of humans who started off with ad-hoc rituals that became more and more elaborate (Marcus 2004). Over a span of 10,000 years this small human population developed a full religion, complete with priests. This knowledge is profound, as it also illustrates our modern religious development.

More than 10,000 years ago, a small parcel of land began to be used by hunters and gatherers during seasons of abundance. The rainy season meant that there was enough food for a few families, numbering perhaps 25-30 people total, to come together for a few months. During the dry seasons, they moved to another site that had more abundant food. Back then, the first site contained a cleared space, measuring about 20 m by 7 m, with two rows of boulders on the sides. The space was kept clean (excavations found debris along on the sides, but not within the cleared space) and was most likely used for rituals watched by the whole group. We have little, if any, evidence to indicate the kind of rituals involved; however, over the next few thousand years, the site and the rituals would evolve significantly.

Soon domesticated maize (corn) evolved to the point where the site was capable of supporting a year-long population 10 times the size of the old one. Some houses appeared; but more importantly, larger buildings, including one serving the rituals (the ritual house) were also constructed. The ritual house is known to be such because it contained a pit used for human sacrifices and benches for the congregation to sit on. The original, simple ad-hoc ritual, in an open space, had evolved to a more complicated version performed at predetermined times, based on a calendar. A few hundred years later, the population swelled to a thousand and began exhibiting hereditary ranks, as seen in the ritual construction (which would have required an organizational hierarchy) and presence of jewelry and other artifacts.

As the chiefs grew in power, the ritual buildings transformed into temples serving the wider community. We find more evidence of ritual, and also greater sophistication in the rituals, which included bloodletting, the sacrifice of enemies, and more.

That culture grew and started to absorb smaller nearby groups and villages. The temples were enlarged with extra rooms, and full-time priests began taking care of both the temples and the ceremonies performed therein. The early, simple set of rituals had become so highly developed that it now had people who committed their entire lives to furthering it and expanding the religion (and the culture itself) according to their own beliefs and convictions. After all, by now they were representing the gods!

The culture abruptly came to an end when a rival group finally destroyed the new state a few centuries later.

Ritual serves the human psyche well. It induces forceful emotions and feelings, particularly if chanting, fire, darkness, and killing are added. In the performance of a ritual, the individuality barrier breaks down; the individual loses his or her identity to become part of a larger group, where all are equal. This creates a sense of group identity and strengthens social bonds. It reaffirms unity, and establishes orderliness and group solidarity by collective activity. Rituals ultimately induce religious experience that becomes so emotional and inspiring that it reinforces belief.

It's no different today. Modern examples of religious rituals include Catholics performing a Mass, or Muslims performing the Friday prayer.

One may ask why ritual is so successful; and the answer is that humans thrive on repetitive and familiar activities, because they provide a sense of comfort and safety. Ritual stimulates the right side of the brain, which responds well to dance, signs, and sounds, and allows one to break through the barrier of logic and critical thought to make contact with the subconscious. As such, ritual has come to serve our religions extremely well. It induces an emotional surge to reinforce the gods and the tenets of the religion, a response so overwhelming that individuals not participating in the ritual may be singled out and even killed.

Today's religions still contain many, many rituals that are used to maintain the loyalty of their respective followers. We may smirk at or be perplexed by the actions of the ancient population described above, but we're not too different. The circumcision practiced by the Egyptians thousands of years ago became part of the Jewish and Islamic religions that are still practiced today. Every major religion has rituals that represent the remains of ancient practices.

Taboo

Taboos, strictly forbidden human/social actions, also became part of our religions. The breaking of a taboo is abhorred by society, and taboos are still very much a part of our present religions, illustrating their descent from ancient religions. Taboo has always existed, but wasn't specifically named as such until the writings of British explorer Captain James Cook became public. When he discovered the island of Tonga, he encountered a race where much of their lives and religion were governed by "tapu" (forbidden) activities; the word "tapu" developed into the modern "taboo." Their observatories and sacred places were declared taboo by the priests sticking small sticks in the ground around them. No man could enter a taboo space unless invited. Cook also observed was that it was taboo for women to eat with the men, and that some food stuffs (such as pork and some fish) were also taboo. Some women had to be fed by others, because they were forbidden to feed themselves for one reason or another; for example, if they had touched a dead body or were menstruating.

There is no society and culture, present or past, which lacks taboos. Typically they vary from culture to culture, though the taboo against incest is prevalent in every society (yet even here, there are exceptions to the rule). It is difficult to trace the origin of specific taboos; some may have started in ancient times for no obvious reasons, simply becoming an unwritten code of laws that got passed from one generation to the next until it was formalized in writing. Some taboos do have reasons: the incest taboo prevents interbreeding, and some cultures originally shunned pork for health reasons. But even when the reason or origin of the taboo is long extinct, it often remains so vigorously enforced that no one will dare violate it.

The anecdote of a probably apocryphal experiment conducted on four gorillas in a cage serves us well here. In the experiment, a ladder is set up against the wall with some appetizing snacks perched on a platform above the ladder. Before long, the first gorilla climbs the ladder to get to the snacks. As he is about to touch them, all the gorillas are sprayed with ice-cold water. Immediately all the gorillas retreat into a corner. Soon, no gorilla will dare go up the ladder; but more significant is the fact that if a gorilla tries to go up the ladder anyway, the other three will forcibly stop him in fear of being sprayed. Then one of the gorillas gets replaced with a new one. As this new gorilla attempts to touch the ladder, the other three will attack him for no apparent reason.

Soon, another newcomer is introduced; and when it tries to get to the treats, it's attacked as well. The previous newcomer participates in the attack, although he has no idea why he is doing it. Soon all the original gorillas are replaced, but the attacks continue because the newcomers have learned that climbing the ladder is taboo. The taboo persists for no apparent reason.

In human societies, the violation of a taboo may result in severe punishment or even death. Even if no one knows why, a sure conviction exists that one will and should be punished for breaking the taboo. He who breaks the taboo will become taboo himself, and in many cases the entire community will condemn and punish this individual to keep the whole community from suffering. This occurs in Jewish and Muslim cultures when individuals break the taboo against eating pork.

The Old Testament records plenty of taboos: for example, against homosexuality. Most Christian countries still enforce this taboo, generally refusing to allow gay marriages (although this is gradually changing). Sexual intercourse during the menstrual period is also a Biblical taboo.

Some taboos may have their origins in actions or objects that caused some harm to a person or society. For protective reasons, the action or object was declared taboo. However, over time, the taboo often became a religious tool used to control people's actions and beliefs. It's taboo to say the name of a deceased person in some cultures (for fear it will draw harmful attention from their spirit), and in today's society, the burning of a Bible is generally feared as a taboo that might bring the revenge of God on all. The destruction of the Quran will surely mean death in a Muslim society.

Modern society is riddled with examples of taboos on topics as varied as nudity, religious beliefs, the plants and animals we may eat, and more. The reasons for many of these taboos are no longer valid, as other methods have been developed to address the relevant issue. However, in many cases the taboos were absorbed into a particular religion; and as such, the religious deity or deities has authority over the taboo, and may punish those who break it—no matter how ridiculous or unreasonable the taboo may be.

Superstition

Superstition comprises a large part of many religious belief systems. Superstition is defined as a belief that some future event can be influenced by an unrelated action. A tennis player may tap his right foot once before serving a ball. A gambler may blow on the dice before throwing them, believing it will increase his chances of winning. A baseball player might wear the same "lucky" socks in every game. The Zulus of Southern Africa once held the superstition that harming or killing the hammerhead bird would bring bad consequences, with the offender's whole village being punished with a violent storm. The same bird was believed by the Hottentot to have the ability to foresee who would die next. If the bird was seen near a house, it might represent a tiding of death.

Ultimately, superstitions are beliefs without scientific proof or reason. So why is superstition so widespread even today, when repeatable, verifiable science underlies and supports most of our society? Surely even in the past, a person performing an action completely unconnected to the outcome of an event would eventually realize that the desired outcome was achieved only rarely (if ever), and give up on the superstition. Obviously, however, this doesn't happen—and the reason can be explained in the theory of reinforcement, which has been proven with both animals and humans.

In 1948, B.F. Skinner discovered superstitious behavior in pigeons. He placed hungry pigeons in a cage, with food delivered at regular intervals with no reference to the pigeon's behavior. However, he found that the pigeons soon associated food delivery with whatever action they were performing when the food was delivered. For example, a bird might turn in one direction or another as food is delivered; wrongly, the bird assumes that the turning induces feeding. So it deliberately begins turning in the same direction. If one of the turns again coincides with a feeding, the bird is now convinced that the turning does indeed induce feeding, and repeats the movement regularly.

Skinner's most important discovery in this series of experiments was the partial reinforcement effect. A pigeon that receives food each time it performs a specific action will eventually forget about the action if the food stops coming. However, a pigeon rewarded with food only now and then when it performs a specific action becomes even more determined and persistent in performing the reaction.

In a modern analogy, a person might believe that he can bring rain by undertaking some action or ritual. If the ritual works once, and then works again a few tries later, then this "rainmaker" will become convinced that this ritual works, and will resist all attempts to convince him otherwise. The belief is now internalized. The "rainmaker" will also find all kinds of reasons why the ritual doesn't work in some cases. Maybe he didn't perform it correctly, or his god was punishing him for something he did. So even whenever a person performs a ritual with the expectation of an outcome, and nothing seems to happen most of the time, it nonetheless develops a sense of persistence within the individual.

Traces of Ancient Practices in Modern Religions
Using our knowledge of the religious practices of isolated communities, in conjunction with archeological evidence, we can construct the building blocks of our present religions. The development was not sequential, but erratic, moving at different rates among different communities. Nonetheless, due to the constants of human behavior, these scattered beginnings had many parallels and similarities. The religious concepts and practices further advanced as these communities came into contact with each other.

Within this mixture of myth, ritual, taboo and superstition, which already included notions of a higher power and an awe for unexplained natural phenomena like day and night, sun and moon, further development took place to connect these concepts. In the ancient religions, animism also prevailed. Animism is the view that everything in the natural world is spiritually alive: i.e. that souls or spirits exist not only in humans, but also in animals, birds, rocks, thunder, mountains, etc. As such, some animals, objects, and phenomena must be treated with respect, in case their spirits decide to take revenge or influence the invisible world. For example, the Hottentot who kills an antelope will perform some ritual or action to appease the spirit of this animal. In some cultures, a mountain might be revered, and a spectacular natural phenomenon such as lightning quickly becomes a god.

Today, we know that distinguishing between the animate (alive) and inanimate (not alive) is an abstraction we develop through learning. In a young child's mind, the whole world around him is alive. A child might feed and provide water for his play animal, for example. Most young children can't distinguish between the natural and human world; and as a matter of fact, neither can adults unless taught. In modern cultures, adults can distinguish between these worlds because they are *taught* to do so; in primitive societies, this distinction does not exist. For example, traditional Australian aborigines believed that the land they lived on is alive, and some still do.

With an attitude like this, it's natural to worship some mountains, plants, or stones, and even later the sun or moon. If one can appease these, often by ritual or sacrifice, one can connect to this unseen world and gain protection or additional power from the associated spirits. Another part of this outlook is that a spirit or soul cannot be killed; it is immune to death in this unseen world. This notion includes human beings. To ensure that the spirit would not harm those left behind— either because it needed to take revenge or was envious of those still alive—rituals were performed and sacrifices made to protect individuals as well as the community from these spirits.

Within this framework, ancestor worship also developed, as still practiced today in many communities within Africa and Asia. So did the concept of the shaman, a person who could serve as a mediator or messenger between the real world and the spirit world. The shaman could also use some of the powers of the spiritual world, e.g. healing. The communication required to enter this spiritual world normally involves some specific ritual and state of mind.

Our First Gods Are Created

Within the human framework of myth, superstition, ritual, and animism, the worshipping of deities (gods) eventually evolved. Such beliefs emerged as a structured way to explain natural phenomena that could not be explained otherwise. The gods, which existed in some mysterious, other world beyond the real, possessed superpowers that could influence the world. They seldom revealed or showed themselves to humans, but their effects could be seen. It soon became normal practice for most religions to use images and symbols to represent these deities.

Having a physical representation of a deity made worshipping and sacrifice easier. The deity could be attributed with powerful characteristics. Ancient religions may have used special stones, trees, birds, or other animals as representations of their deities. As tool-making and art evolved, it became possible to shape an object or otherwise create a physical image to represent the deity; and thus our first gods came into true physical being. This heralded the era of the plethora of gods that has pervaded the prehistory and history of humankind.

But eventually, these gods—no matter how powerful—were replaced by even more powerful deities, their power supported and stimulated by the beliefs of millions or billions of people.

These religious transformations occurred in a fashion similar to that of the nomad population in Mexico, which settled down and advanced from simple ritual to a formal religion before being wiped out by competitors. The human populations progressively grew in size, and all that goes with it: the ability to invent, the ability to adapt, a talent for survival. Numbers began to multiply, first slowly and then exponentially. As a result, the shift from hunter-gatherers to cultivator-harvesters began. Horticulture, and later agriculture, required far more work but also produced far more food.

Human life ways evolved from nomadic wandering to basic settlement, first part-time and then full-time, to agricultural village, to city, and then to state. With this transformation, specialization of labor developed. Farmers were transformed into builders, artisans, dealers, soldiers, and priests. Social stratification developed, with peasant farmers at the bottom and the ruling class at the top. With this development, religion also transformed from the ad-hoc rituals, superstition, magic, myths and first deities into state religions.

As religion was the link between this world and the unknown/unseen other world of nature and death the ruling class became the guardians of religion. Either the priests came to rule, or royalty came to rule with the support of the priests. The assumption was that if you were a ruler, then a god must favor you; and so you needed, in return, to favor that god, and rule on his divine behalf. Therefore, followers must follow both the god and the human ruler.

As these societies became more complex, religion and belief also became more complex. This transformation into powerful states started approximately 3,300 BCE with some of the biggest states arising in:

- Mesopotamia
- Egypt
- The Indus River Valley
- Northern China
- The Niger River Valley
- Central Mexico
- The Andes Mountains

Interestingly, most of these states formed in regions of scarce resources, where people were forced to cooperate in order to maximize their chances of survival. Few examples are as striking as ancient Egypt. The fertile Nile River provided a reliable source of water and other resources in a region that was not otherwise easily survivable.

The ever-increasing human population and struggle for resources meant that the humans who congregated in the Nile Valley hastened their transformation from nomadic life ways into a village, then city, and finally state-level culture. The Egyptian religion developed along with the increasing elaborate society, eventually consisting of a multitude of deities for all things large and small, as well as an associated underworld.

In ancient Greece, also a relatively arid region near the Mediterranean Ocean, the familiar pantheon of Greek gods and their mythology developed (much of which was subsumed into the belief systems of their Roman inheritors). Mesopotamian religion also presented a wide range of gods and practices, many associated with a specific city or city-state. In general, the religions of humankind accelerated in their development, exploding in a multitude of beliefs and ritual.

This is where our story of modern-day religion truly starts. The next chapter lays out the evolution of these proto-religions into the religions of today.

CHAPTER 2

The Era of the Gods

Not for one moment can I believe that the only purpose of the world and the universe is to serve as a vast playground for a god or gods, as humans worship them, begging for redemption.

The Ancient Nomads Who Conceived God

Between 1,700 and 1,300 BCE, a story played out that profoundly changed the religious journey of humankind. The setting of this story was none other than a dry, barren landscape wedged between the fertile Nile Valley and the equally fertile valleys of the Tigris and Euphrates rivers—an area better known as Mesopotamia. This region was to become the birthplace of many of our modern gods, and certainly of the god who, by several names, has come to dominate the cultures of the Western world.

By 1,700 BCE, the Nile Valley was under the tight control of the Egyptian dynasties. Mesopotamia, further north, was ruled by the powerful Babylonians. Between these two countries stretched an arid region where several nomadic tribes made a very basic living. Archeological evidence tracks the development of humans in this area from a basic hunter-gatherer society 18,000-10,000 BCE into an agricultural society by 12,500-9,500 BCE, with some small villages with labor specialization appearing in the period 8,500-4,300 BCE.

The proto-Hebrews emerged no earlier than about 1,700 BCE and no later than 1,300 BCE, possibly when smaller tribes banded together for survival. They were either Semitic people who migrated to the area from Southern Arabia, or a composite splinter group composed of existing Semitic and Mediterranean peoples. They were nomadic, with a polytheistic religion consisting of many gods interwoven with myth, superstition, and ritual. Gradual climate change associated with the end of the last Ice Age, thousands of years before, made survival in the area between Egypt and Mesopotamia increasingly difficult, and things became drier and drier over the centuries. Parkland and woodland faded into desert, with the few remaining fertile spots taken and ruled by the strongest.

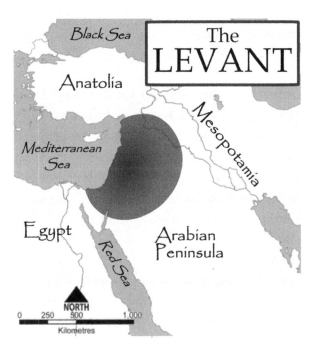

Figure 2: The Levant, a dry and barren landscape between the fertile Nile Valley and Mesopotamia.

Those tribes outside the remaining fertile regions were slowly pushed toward starvation, and the Hebrews were no exception.

Thus marginalized and living on meager resources, the Hebrews were forced to move closer to Egypt in search of better grazing for their livestock. It was in the subsequent contact between a simple nomadic tribe and the advanced Egyptian civilization and religion that the origins of the Abrahamic religions of Judaism, Christianity, and Islam (in the order of their advent) can be found. The Hebrews were to swap their political autonomy for access to resources. In the process, they lost their self-determination, and found their own religion and culture threatened and influenced by the powerful Egyptian gods and the Nile region's sophisticated culture.

It is here that we pick up the story in the Bible, to trace the transformation of the Hebrew belief structure from a belief in many gods (polytheism) to profound belief in a single god (monotheism).

The Hebrews lived on the borders of Egypt—and at the time, Egypt was using slaves to build its ever increasing state. The older brothers of one Hebrew family committed the ultimate sin when, being jealous of the attention their father (Jacob) lavished on his youngest son (Joseph, of the coat of many colors), they sold him to a camel caravan carrying spices and perfumes to Egypt. Once in Egypt, Joseph was sold to Potiphar, the captain of the Pharaoh's guard. Hard-working as he was, he gained the trust of his master, with ever increasing responsibility assigned to him until he became overseer of Potiphar's whole household. He also came to the attention of Potiphar's wife; she desired him, and sought an affair.

Joseph rejected her advances, so she falsely accused him of forcing himself upon her, and he was thrown in prison. Soon afterward, the cupbearer and chief baker of the Pharaoh were also thrown in prison, as they had offended the Pharaoh. Both of them had unusual dreams, and they asked Joseph to interpret them. Joseph told them that the chief baker would be hanged and the cupbearer would return to duty, which indeed came to pass. Once back on duty, the cupbearer called upon Joseph to help the Pharaoh understand one of the Pharaoh's dreams.

Joseph interpreted the Pharaoh's dream as indicating that seven years of abundance would be followed by seven years of famine, and advised the Pharaoh to store surplus grain. Recognizing the wisdom of Joseph's advice, the Pharaoh appointed Joseph to oversee the storage of surplus grain. When famine struck, Egypt had more than enough supplies on hand, and the Pharaoh amassed more wealth by selling the surplus grain to others who needed it. During the famine, Joseph's brothers visited Egypt to buy grain. Forgiving them, Joseph used his influence to allow the Hebrew tribe to settle in prosperous Egypt.

The Bible states in Exodus:

> 6 And Joseph died, and all his brethren, and all that generation.
> 7 And the children of Israel were fruitful, and increased abundantly, and multiplied, and waxed exceeding mighty; and the land was filled with them.

The presence of the Hebrew people in such numbers, with their own political aspirations, became a threat for the Egyptians. However, by then they were so integrated into the Egyptian economy that the Pharaoh couldn't let them go. To stem the increasing Hebrew population, the Pharaoh issued a decree that all male Hebrew babies were to be killed. The horror of this atrocity had a profound and devastating effect on the Hebrew nation, kindling the embers of a dream to leave Egypt and reclaim the land where they had originated: A promised land where they could again have self-determination and political freedom.

The Hebrew group had a strong sense of identity, but more importantly, they had their own gods—which were different from the Egyptian gods. We can only speculate as to the number and names of all their gods then, as the record is muddled. We know from archaeological evidence that the supreme god in the Levant/Canaan religions back then was El, father of humankind and all creatures. El may have originated as a thunder or sky god. When the Hebrew tribe was forced to move away from their land, they also moved away from their places of worship. Where previously they may have associated their gods with places, locations, or objects, they now only had images of these gods in their collective memory. Over time, the original seen and tangible gods evolved into abstract versions of themselves.

We find some reference to the gods of the Hebrew tribe in the Bible. When Moses led the Hebrews out of Egypt and went up the mountain to revere his God, the tribe got tired of waiting for him to return and cast a golden calf as one of their gods. If one accepts the Biblical accounts as true, then at this stage the Hebrew people were still polytheistic in nature, and easily returned to this tendency. The Hebrew people yearned for a leader to lead them out of Egypt. Soon Moses will fulfill this task as told by the Bible.

While the Hebrew presence in ancient Egypt remains an article of Jewish and Christian faith, to date no archaeological evidence has been recovered in Egypt that indicates a Hebrew presence at any time. Neither are there any references to the Hebrews in any Egyptian records of the period. The closest is the term "Habiri," used in some Egyptian texts, that referred to semi-nomadic rebels or bandits who settled in Egypt. The word Hebrew may also stem from the word "eber," meaning "other side" or "beyond," as they were identified as "the people on the other side of the river."

We're left with the notion that the Biblical story of the Hebrews in Egypt is either a myth, or that the Hebrew tribe was so insignificant to the Egyptians that it was not considered worth recording.

The Birth of a New God (Judaism)

Moses himself is an individual so cloaked in myth and antiquity that it's difficult to separate truth from fiction. According to the story, he was born during the period of the royal decree requiring the death of all male Hebrew babies. Knowing that the baby would be killed if the Egyptian soldiers found him, his mother made a reed basket for him, and laid him on the river. From Exodus:

> *3 And when she could no longer hide him, she took for him an ark of bulrushes, and daubed it with slime and with pitch; and she put the child therein, and laid it in the flags by the river's brink.*

5 And the daughter of Pharaoh came down to bathe at the river; and her maidens walked along by the river-side; and she saw the ark among the flags, and sent her handmaid to fetch it.

6 And she opened it, and saw the child: and, behold, the babe wept. And she had compassion on him, and said, this is one of the Hebrews' children.

7 Then said her sister to Pharaoh's daughter, Shall I go and call thee a nurse of the Hebrew women, that she may nurse the child for thee?

This is the start of the story of Moses, who would later profoundly define the three Abrahamic religions: a slave child who was raised in the Pharaoh's house with the best education and luxuries the Egyptian palace could offer. A child given all the knowledge of his oppressors, but a child who was very much aware that he was one of the oppressed, and an outcast as a result.

How much of the story of Moses' origin is true, how much myth? The story of a child who is threatened and then raised by animals or poor people far from his true parents is quite common in legends; this is a unique twist, of course, given that Moses' adoptive parents were the richest and most powerful in the land. In most of these legends, the child discovers his heritage as an adult, and then takes vengeance to attain greatness or become a leader. The story of Moses is very similar to the myth of Sargon of Agade, the founder of Babylon, who was also put in a basket and laid on the river and then found by Akki, the drawer of water. Sargon was first a gardener, later becoming a King who ruled for 45 years.

In their early years, many children also cherish the myth that one day, they'll discover that they come from noble parentage, and then will rise up to take revenge against those who wronged them and/or become powerful rulers. It is also well understood that most of our past heroes and leaders have an abundance of myth surrounding their births and upbringings. Otto Rank (1909), looking at the literary history of a various cultures, concluded :

Almost all important civilized peoples have early woven myths around and glorified in poetry of their heroes, mythical kings and princes, founders of religions, of dynasties, empires and cities—in short, their national heroes. Especially the history of their birth and of their early years is furnished with fantasy traits; the amazing similarity, nay, literal identity of those tales, even if they refer to different completely independent people, sometimes geographically far removed from one another, is well known.

Being raised in the Pharaoh's palace, Moses had the advantage of an Egyptian education. But he was still a Hebrew boy, a boy who knew he came from a slave race, an oppressed race. Moses also had a Hebrew nanny who would have nurtured the Jewish dream of freedom. History tells us that many of our freedom fighters came from backgrounds in which they were educated by the oppressor. So the seeds were already sown in Moses regarding the aspirations and dreams of his people.

What was the religion of the Hebrew people at the time of the Pharaohs, and what was the religion of the Egyptians? Can we find any clues to today's gods in these two religions? To cast further light on modern gods, we need to consider the two religions.

The Egyptian Religion

The religion of the ancient Egyptians is fairly well illustrated in their artwork and artifacts. It was a religion based on as many as 2,000 gods and goddesses, deities who had evolved from their previous religious backgrounds of animism, myth, and superstition. Egypt was beset with religion, which guided most, if not all, aspects of everyday life. Some of the gods were worshipped throughout the whole country, some only locally.

The two main gods, however, were Amon-Ra and Osiris. Amon-Ra was the sun god and lord of the universe. Osiris was the god of the underworld, who made a peaceful afterlife possible. The Egyptians were infatuated by the idea of life after death, and this concept dominated their religion. Numerous Temples were constructed for the gods, and were considered their actual dwelling places. Each city had a Temple built for the god of its city, which served as a place to communicate with the god. The Temples had priests who looked after the Temple, and being "close" to the god, these priests also became very powerful.

The Egyptian religion may seem strange and mystical to modern eyes, but the belief in an afterlife, a powerful god, and a Temple or place to worship is little different from our own religious practices today.

The Gods of the Hebrew Nation

The original religion of the Hebrews was similar to those of the other nomadic tribes in the wilderness between Egypt and Mesopotamia, consisting of animistic and natural phenomena worshipped as gods. The Egyptian gods were busy looking after the well-being of the Egyptians, their royal family, and their military power, so the Hebrew nation needed their own gods to look after them. The clash between the Egyptians and Hebrews, therefore, was also a clash between their gods. The Hebrew gods had to help the Hebrew nation find their own country and self-determination.

Moses was educated in the Pharaoh's palace in the philosophy, beliefs, and rituals of the Egyptians, while his Hebrew nanny taught him about the Hebrew gods and beliefs. Moses straddled two worlds: the complex Egyptian world, and the primordial Hebrew world. To make sense of these worlds, Moses had to reconcile the two belief systems.

Moses used his knowledge of Egyptian gods and beliefs to further advance and define the Hebrew gods. There are even strong suggestions that Moses might have been an Egyptian priest or altar boy at some point, as his later religious rituals very much resembled some Egyptian religious practices.

Moses and the One God

The greatest change that Moses was to bring to his world was monotheism, the belief in one supreme god. This was a profound change for that region of the world; previously, many gods had been allowed to exist more or less peacefully together, but Moses was to preach that there was one and only one god to be followed, a jealous god, a god exclusively for the Hebrews—a god who would help the Hebrew nation conquer all others. But where did this sudden Supreme Being come from? There are several possibilities:

1. The Hebrew religion had already evolved to recognize only one god by the time Moses arrived on the scene;

2. A sect developed in the Hebrew religion, originating with Abraham (one of the ancient ancestors of the Hebrew nation) that believed in one god;

3. Moses himself came to the conclusion that there was only one god, and that all others were false;

4. Moses was educated in the short-lived era when the pharaoh Akhenaten introduced the concept of one god, influencing Moses' belief system;

5. The idea of one god was developed later, and retroactively applied to history by a Hebrew priest or group of priests advocating one god.

The concept of a single, all-powerful god was also introduced by the Egyptian Pharaoh Akhenaten during his reign, when he declared the god Aten as the state god. Other gods were abolished, their images smashed, their names excised from monuments and written records, their temples abandoned, and their revenues impounded. The plural for "god" was suppressed. There was to be only one god, and no one was to even consider the possibility of more than one.

Was Moses actually raised during this radical religious transformation in Egypt, or at least raised in an Egyptian household that still held this belief? After the death of Akhenaten, most of the Egyptians returned to their old ways and previous beliefs. Indeed, it was the god Aten who was expunged this time, his images destroyed and his inscriptions removed. The transformation from polytheism to monotheism proved to be too radical for the Egyptian civilization to accept.

One thing that was distinctive to the Egyptian religions was that the Pharaoh considered himself to be the direct representative of a god, and therefore the mediator between the common man and that god. The rule of the Pharaoh was therefore by divine order; and so resistance to the Pharaoh is seen as disobedience to the gods. The divine rule of the Pharaoh went further; the Pharaoh was no longer considered the son of his father and mother, but rather the son of his mother and the god.

Having a god as the national leader allows the transition of the supernatural, divine world to the human world. A thousand years later, Jesus Christ went through a similar transformation: he was no longer the son of Mary and Joseph, but the son of Mary and the Hebrew God. God had fertilized Mary to bring this half man/half god (demigod) to Earth, much as the Greek gods often did to women themselves, producing many of the classical heroes such as Hercules and Perseus.

Moses, with his superior education and knowledge, became a revolutionary for the Hebrews, a leader with a vision to free his own people. But even more importantly, Moses had come to accept the vision of only one god, and an abstract god at that. Witnessing one day the beating of a Hebrew man by an Egyptian overseer, he killed the overseer in a moment of rage. Fearing for his life, he fled the empire. Moses was now banished to a simple life of hardship, isolated from the sophisticated Egyptian culture. He still nurtured the dream of freeing his people from their slavery and suffering. During this time of isolation, Moses must have furthered and advanced the concept of his god: a god exclusively for the Hebrews, a god to free them forever.

Once the Pharaoh passed away, it became safe for Moses to return to Egypt; and during that period, a series of events (almost certainly myths), got interwoven with Hebrew history. The Bible tells us that God ordered Moses, from a burning bush, to return to Egypt to free the Hebrew nation. Once in Egypt, Moses and his brother Aaron approached the new Pharaoh, asking him to allow the Hebrew nation to leave Egypt. The Pharaoh refused, and the Hebrew God then took revenge by sending a series of plagues ranging from frogs, lice, flies, death of livestock, boils, hail, locusts, and darkness to convince the Pharaoh otherwise. Even so, the Pharaoh refused.

But there was still one more horror left: Moses' God would kill all the firstborn children of the Egyptians, including the firstborn of all livestock. (Why any god would want to kill innocent children is beyond me). The first myths of the power of Moses' god were in the making. From Exodus 11:

4 And Moses said, Thus said Jehovah, about midnight will I go out into the midst of Egypt:

5 And all the first-born in the land of Egypt shall die, from the first-born of Pharaoh that sit upon his throne, even unto the first-born of the maid-servant that is behind the mill; and all the first-born of cattle.

6 And there shall be a great cry throughout all the land of Egypt, such as there hath not been, nor shall be any more.

29 And it came to pass at midnight, that Jehovah smote all the first-born in the land of Egypt, from the first-born of Pharaoh that sat on his throne unto the first-born of the captive that was in the dungeon; and all the first-born of cattle.

30 And Pharaoh rose up in the night, he, and all his servants, and all the Egyptians; and there was a great cry in Egypt, for there was not a house where there was not one dead.

Despite this Biblical claim, to this very day no evidence has been found in the Egyptian writings referring to the above events. There may have been a splinter group of the Hebrews who left Egypt at that time, but if so, it was an event so minor that no attention was paid to it by the Egyptians. The plagues and later escape by Moses and his people through the Red Sea can only be seen as myths.

In any case: as the story has it, after the atrocity of the killing of all the first-borns by the avenging God, the Pharaoh agreed to allow the Hebrews to leave. The next few years were to define Moses and the later Jewish religion. The small religious sect under the command of Moses entered the barren landscape surrounding Egypt in search of the Promised Land. Using God and the pledge of a better life, Moses was eventually able to maintain a strong hold on his wandering tribe.

Moses went about imposing a new religion: one he had already devised, but a religion new to his people. The desolate landscape that the Jews entered was hostile and difficult to survive in, so he had to keep his followers content and stifle any dissent. Moses promised his people that God would look after them, and the expectations of his people were high. Arriving at the foot of Mount Sinai, Moses ordered his people not to touch the mountain, to wash themselves, and to abstain from sexual intercourse for three days. At this mountain, Moses was to lay the foundations for his religion. On the early morning of the third day, the Hebrew camp was covered by a cloud, and God revealed Himself through thunder and lightning, and coming down in a cloud of His own. He dictated to them the Ten Commandments, including instructions that they would have no god before Him, that no idols or "graven images" were allowed, that they should follow the Sabbath and keep it holy, and more.

He also instructed them to build an altar for offers to Him, and laid down a host of other instructions, ranging from killing any sorceress or person caught performing bestiality to killing anyone sacrificing to any other god than He. Through God, Moses ordered the construction of an ark of acacia wood, with a Tabernacle to house it, including a courtyard. The Tabernacle was a place of worship with priests appointed by Moses to look after it.

Moses had now set the cornerstones of his beliefs. He defined:

1. A set of laws to live by.
2. A place of worship.
3. The presence of an Almighty God as the ultimate authority.

Moses then went up onto Mount Sinai for 40 days—a period during which his religion was quickly challenged, showing the tenacity of the old religion. In his absence the Hebrew tribe convinced Aaron (his brother) to make a golden calf by collecting gold rings, melting them down, and recasting them into the idol. This was a direct challenge to the religious transformation of Moses.

On his return, Moses was furious to find his new religion cast aside, with all his beliefs threatened. This was to become a turning point in the religious history of humanity, as Moses was to finally end the era of many gods and introduce the concept of a single and Almighty God. As with so many other abrupt changes in world history, it would require murder and blood to silence the dissenters.

Moses called together all those who still believed in his teachings, commanding them to kill all those who had violated or might have violated his religion, regardless of whether they were brothers, friends, or neighbors. He and his followers moved through the camp methodologically, putting all dissenters to the sword, in a murderous religious cleansing, clearly recorded in Exodus 32:

> 26 *Then Moses stood in the gate of the camp, and said, who is on Jehovah's side, let him come unto me. And all the sons of Levi gathered themselves together unto him.*
>
> 27 *And he said unto them, Thus said Jehovah, the god of Israel, Put every man his sword upon his thigh, and go to and fro from gate to gate throughout the camp, and slay every man his brother, and every man his companion, and every man his neighbor.*
>
> 28 *And the sons of Levi did according to the word of Moses: and there fell of the people that day about three thousand men.*

One might have thought the simple appearance of the Hebrew god would have been enough to convince the Hebrew people to follow him. But Moses was fanatical and could allow no dissention at all; his god, the one he perceived, would rule at all cost. All those believing in other gods, even the old Hebrew gods, were murdered.

The God of Moses

Four themes of the developing Jewish religion deserve a closer examination here:

1. Moses as leader.
2. The appearance of God.
3. Sacrificing to God.
4. The construction of the Ark of the Covenant.

Let's start with Moses, and see if we can determine what made him such an effective leader that he earned a historic place in our religions. There are remarkable similarities between the leadership of Moses and the leadership of modern cults. One of the most extreme cults witnessed in modern times was the religious group that called itself the Branch Davidians.

The group was led by a man called David Koresh, who believed himself to be the final prophet. Koresh claimed he was the son of God, and God's tool to bring justice and God's reign to the world. Within a relatively few years, he built a community of fanatical believers and followers. Teaching a strict version of the Bible and his own interpretation of Christianity, he was worshipped and admired by his flock. His stranglehold was so tight that they chose death over surrender when confronted by law officers and legal agencies.

Subsequent studies of cults, especially extreme cases that led to mass suicide, have identified the following characteristics that most (if not all) hold in common:

- **A Single Authority:** The cult leader is the absolute authoritarian, and makes all the decisions himself. He believes himself to be the only one who can make the right decisions.
- **Unconditional trust:** Extreme loyalty is demanded, with unquestioning faith. No criticism of the leader is tolerated.
- **Shaky credentials:** Most such leaders are self-appointed experts, often self-educated, if educated at all.
- **Claims of direct contact to God:** Since he speaks on God's behalf, the leader can't be questioned or argued with.
- **Promises of greatness:** The cult members are the Chosen Ones, and will change or inherit the world. They will be regarded in the future as those who saved the world.
- **Claims of evil temptations:** The leader declares that anyone not following him is evil or comes from the devil, threatening the good and right.
- **Claims of a big event coming:** Most of the cults claim that a large-scale religious event will soon occur, and that the flock

must be patient and keep believing. All the suffering will be worthwhile in the end.

- **Sexual abuse and/or child rape:** Many cult leaders have sex with many of their followers, including young girls. It is considered the right of the leader and a privilege for the girl.

Ultimately, the cult leader creates an exclusive and elitist society, cut off from the mainstream. Everyone else is viewed as being an outsider, and therefore inferior—perhaps even subhuman. An examination of Moses, based on Biblical scripture, doesn't differ much from the above characteristics. For Moses, the Hebrew tribe provided fertile soil for his rise to leadership. Oppressed and with no political identity, the Hebrews were ripe for someone to come along and free them. A leader promising a land of milk and honey, self-determination, and a god mightier than all other gods was compelling, and they blindly adopted Moses as their ruler.

Let's compare Moses with our above list; you'll note that he exhibits the majority of the above characteristics. He was (1) the single authority making decisions for his people. (2) He claimed to have direct contact with God, thereby forcing his will and decisions on everyone. Every now and then, Moses would go up a mountain and, in a cloud of smoke and thunder, return with a new message from God. (3) He promised the Hebrews that they would rule the world and all other nations. (4) He claimed the evils of other gods and the devil affected those who disbelieved in his teachings, to keep people from straying from him. (5) He used the big event of finally settling down in a land with abundant resources as a carrot to ensure his followers would endure all the hardships they faced meanwhile—and would continue to do so as long as necessary.

Moses murdered and plundered repeatedly in the name of his god. There are many more such atrocities recorded in the Bible. From Numbers:

32 And while the children of Israel were in the wilderness, they found a man gathering sticks upon the Sabbath day.

33 And they that found him gathering sticks brought him unto Moses and Aaron, and unto the entire congregation.
34 And they put him in ward, because it had not been declared what should be done to him.
35 And Jehovah said unto Moses, The man shall surely be put to death: the entire congregation shall stone him with stones without the camp.
36 And all the congregation brought him without the camp, and stoned him to death with stones; as Jehovah commanded Moses.

The madness of Moses had no end. Once, after plundering another country, his followers killed all the men, and the soldiers brought back the women and children. Moses was furious that the women and children were spared. Again, from Numbers:

14 And Moses was wroth with the officers of the host, the captains of thousands and the captains of hundreds, who came from the service of the war.
15 And Moses said unto them, have ye saved all the women alive?
16 Behold, these caused the children of Israel, through the counsel of Balaam, to commit trespass against Jehovah in the matter of Peor, and so the plague was among the congregation of Jehovah.
17 Now therefore kill every male among the little ones, and kill every woman that has known man by lying with him.
18 But all the women-children, that have not known man by lying with him, keep alive for yourselves.

What an atrocity! The fearful women and children were herded to the Hebrew camp. They must have been crying, begging for their lives. Moses ordered all the male children to be murdered in front of their mothers, and then had the women killed. Only the young girls survived, and they were given to the soldiers for their pleasure. Where was the Hebrew God now? Moses killed, murdered, and raped in his name.

I'll give you my take on Moses: He was a psychopath who killed and plundered using a god he either created himself, or adopted from the Egyptians or one of the gods already worshipped by the Hebrews. For 40 years, he quenched his thirst for power with a tribe he manipulated to the extreme. Moses never had any intention of reaching the Promised Land.

But what about the appearances of God to the tribe of Moses? How did this happen? In the description in Exodus and Leviticus, God is depicted several times as coming down to Earth in a cloud of smoke and thunder. Let us go back to the Egyptians, where Moses was raised. Modern study and understanding of the Egyptian priesthood and their rituals provide many insights into the rites and God of Moses. The Egyptian temples had a courtyard for the ordinary people to meet within, leading to an inner courtyard. From there, the floor sloped upwards to the inner sanctuary, with diminishing light along the way. Incense and smoke filled the air as one approached the altar of the god, typically located in a dark room. From a small passage at the back, the priest could approach the altar, and with a mixture of stage magic and sounds would deliver his rites and teachings.

The appearance of God unto the Hebrew people was quite similar. Moses used his knowledge of Egyptian rites and rituals, which the Hebrews did not know of, to create his own God Show.

As previously mentioned, there is a strong possibility that Moses served either as a priest or altar boy in one of the many Egyptian temples. Using the same techniques and mixture of magic and charms, he made a god seem to appear in a cloud of smoke and thunder to keep his people believing. The temple Moses ordered built for his people and the ark was similar to the Egyptian temples, with the material and layout almost the same, except that it was adapted to be mobile. An altar was used for offerings similar to those offerings made by the Egyptian priests to their gods. Moses introduced a complete code of sacrificing to God, along with a dress code; what could be offered to God; the way it must be offered; and how much should be left to the priests. This was a highly effective copy of the Egyptian religion, used to awe the Hebrew tribe and keep them following Moses's own god. An example of a Hebrew sacrifice described in Leviticus illustrates the sacrificial scheme well.

6 And if his oblation (offering) for a sacrifice of peace-offerings unto Jehovah be of the flock, male or female, he shall offer it without blemish.
8 and he shall lay his hand upon the head of his oblation (offering), and kill it before the tent of meeting: and Aaron's sons shall sprinkle the blood thereof upon the altar round about.
9 And he shall offer of the sacrifice of peace-offerings an offering made by fire unto Jehovah; the fat thereof, the fat tail entire, he shall take away hard by the backbone; and the fat that cover the inwards, and all the fat that is upon the inwards,
11 And the priest shall burn it upon the altar: it is the food of the offering made by fire unto Jehovah.

As with many modern cults, women earned special attention in the cult of Moses. The cleansing of an unfaithful wife is described in Numbers:

11 And Jehovah spoke unto Moses, saying,
12 Speak unto the children of Israel, and say unto them, if any man's wife go astray, and commit a trespass against him,
13 and a man lie with her carnally, and it be hid from the eyes of her husband, and be kept close, and she be defiled, and there be no witness against her, and she be not taken in the act;
14 and the spirit of jealousy come upon him, and he is jealous of his wife, and she is defiled: or if the spirit of jealousy comes upon him, and he is jealous of his wife, and she is not defiled:
15 then shall the man bring his wife unto the priest, and shall bring her oblation for her, the tenth part of an ephah of barley meal; he shall pour no oil upon it, nor put frankincense thereon; for it is a meal-offering of jealousy, a meal-offering of memorial, bringing iniquity to remembrance.
16 And the priest shall bring her near, and set her before Jehovah:
18 And the priest shall set the woman before Jehovah, and let the hair of the woman's head go loose, and put the meal-offering of memorial in her hands, which is the meal-offering of jealousy: and the priest shall have in his hand the water of bitterness that cause the curse.

19 And the priest shall cause her to swear, and shall say unto the woman, If no man have lain with thee, and if thou have not gone aside to uncleanness, being under thy husband, be thou free from this water of bitterness that cause the curse.

20 But if thou have gone aside, being under thy husband, and if thou are defiled, and some man has lain with thee besides thy husband:

21 then the priest shall cause the woman to swear with the oath of cursing, and the priest shall say unto the woman, Jehovah make thee a curse and an oath among thy people, when Jehovah doth make thy thigh to fall away, and thy body to swell;

22 and this water that cause the curse shall go into thy bowels, and make thy body to swell, and thy thigh to fall away. And the woman shall say, Amen, Amen.

27 And when he hath made her drink the water, then it shall come to pass, if she be defiled, and have committed a trespass against her husband, that the water that cause the curse shall enter into her and become bitter, and her body shall swell, and her thigh shall fall away: and the woman shall be a curse among her people.

How many women got fearfully dragged to the priest to be cleansed or killed, with no one able to come to their aid? Sobbing and fearful, an accused woman would be left alone in the dark with the priest, the altar smoking with the smell of burned meat. The priest would then perform some ritual to his liking and satisfaction. Humiliating and terrifying the hapless victim, the priest would either cleanse or kill her to satisfy his lust. This was no place for a god; it was a place of horror. The rituals performed were not much different from those of a cult where the women are suppressed and used for sexual purposes. The above treatment of women also set the stage for the oppressed status of women in today's religions, where they are often regarded as inherently sinful.

After Moses died, the Hebrew leadership was passed to Joshua, who was tasked with leading the Hebrew tribe into the Promised Land. He did. A long history of feuds and wars with neighboring countries followed, as recorded in the Bible—a history soaked in blood and misery, as the Hebrews murdered and plundered all those around them, or got murdered and plundered by others.

Among other things, the Bible records an incident in which the Israelites, after conquering a village, lined up all the survivors alongside a length of rope. They then killed two of the three resulting groups, allowing the third to survive to work as slaves. In another battle, one of the Hebrew chiefs (Jephthah) fighting on behalf of Israel promised God that if he won the battle, he would sacrifice and give to God the first person he met on his return home. In Judges 11:

> *31 Then it shall be that whatsoever cometh forth from the doors of my house to meet me, when I return in peace from the children of Ammon, it shall be Jehovah's, and I will offer it up for a burnt-offering.*

Jephthah won the battle—and it turned out that his beloved daughter met him upon his return. But a promise is a promise: Jephthah's daughter was sacrificed and burned. Her only sin was to meet her father after his return from the war.

Moses's God produced a world of atrocity and horror in His name.

The Hebrew tribe would resettle in the Levant with some success, although the struggle for resources and land never ended. Battle after battle took place; and although Moses and his followers advocated a single God throughout this period, there is evidence that the Hebrew people still had many gods even then. Later, as their wealth and reputation for excellent workmanship increased, they attracted the attention of King Nebuchadnezzar of Persia, who attacked the Hebrew tribe to enslave and transport them to Babylon. The Jewish nation and its temple were destroyed. Many generations later, a new King released them and allowed them to return to Jerusalem, where they continued to develop their faith, and constructed a new temple.

What Did the Hebrew God Look Like?

The concept and image of the Hebrew God evolved further during the Hebrew exile in Babylon. But what were the attributes of this God that Moses had created, either by adapting one of the Egyptian gods or a previous Hebrew god? The Old Testament of the Bible tells us this about the Hebrew God:

1. He was a God of reward and punishment. If you followed Moses's orders and directions, you were awarded; if you did not, or turned against his God, you were severely punished.
2. He was a God who required sacrifices to be pleased.
3. He was a God for the Hebrew nation only. He would protect the Hebrews and lead them to victory.
4. He was the *only* god. No other gods were allowed.
5. Only men were allowed to be seen or to serve God in the temple.
6. He was a new god who could not be represented by an image or idol.
7. He was omnipresent and omnipotent.
8. He could make anything change or happen.

After the destruction of the Second Temple, the Hebrew nation never recovered. Most of the Hebrews migrated to other countries, or were absorbed into other cultures. Their strong religious code and beliefs, however, meant the survival of the Jewish belief system in these scattered communities. The dream of the Chosen Nation of God and the coming salvation of God remains alive to this day. Despite the deplorable onslaught against the Jewish peoples throughout the ages, in which they were persecuted and murdered with little or no impunity, the Jewish religion survived. Its greatest legacy, however, is arguably the other religions that arose from it—to become its greatest theological rivals, and some of the most widespread belief systems in the modern world.

Judaism Today

Judaism is still very much alive, still steeped in the beliefs that Moses and his successors developed and spread thousands of years ago. Modern synagogues are quite similar to the ancient temples of worship that travelled with the nomadic Hebrews, though of course they're fixed today. The ancient teachings of Moses are still followed, including many of the ancient rituals. Ultimately, these are old Egyptian rituals that were adapted by Moses to fit his needs. The sacred writings of the Jewish religion are contained in the Torah (a.k.a. the Hebrew Bible). The Torah consists of two parts, namely the Written Torah and the Oral Torah, with the written Torah consisting of three parts consisting of:

1. The Pentateuch, the five books of the written Torah dictated to Moses on Mount Sinai by God approximately 3,500 years ago.
2. Prophets, the chronicles of God's direct words to his later prophets.
3. Writings, the books written by the prophets under the guidance of God.

Today, we have strong evidence that the written Torah was not completed any earlier than 539-334 BCE (as opposed to the religious notion that the revelation of the Torah to Moses occurred in 1,380 BCE, as calculated according to the holy texts). The evidence shows that, like the Christian Bible, the Torah is most likely a synthesis of documents from a small number of originally independent sources, the product of many authors and minds over the course of centuries. It reached its final accepted composition around the 6th and 5th centuries BCE. The Jewish religion as practiced now appears to consist of the inventions of many authors, who each added his own story and convictions to the original tale.

The Oral Torah consists of explanations of the Written Torah passed down verbally from generation to generation. After the destruction of the Temple in Jerusalem, and with most of the Hebrew nation scattered, the Oral Torah was written down so that it would not be forgotten. Many variants of the Jewish religion exist today, which is no surprise, given that Jewish groups developed different beliefs and interpretations in their isolated communities after they fled persecution. Five main branches of Judaism developed in this way:

1. Orthodox Judaism
2. Conservative Judaism
3. Reform Judaism
4. Reconstructionist Judaism
5. Humanistic Judaism

Most Jews are still waiting for the Messiah, who will lead the world to peace with the Hebrew God as the one and only god. Christianity and Islam are not accepted as valid; nor is Jesus considered the Messiah, or Muhammad God's prophet.

Like Ra, the ancient Egyptian sun god, the Hebrew god has now fallen silent. But two influential religions arose out of the Hebrew beliefs: the aforementioned Christianity and Islam. Next we'll take a look at the Christian god, who developed out of the Hebrew God via the teachings of an itinerant preacher about 2,000 years ago.

Jesus and His God

We've now seen how an ancient god of a Jewish tribe (or possibly a borrowed Egyptian god) was transformed by Moses into the God of the Jews. This same god was to be transformed again to become a god for the gentiles (non-believers) who lived amongst the Jewish tribes in Palestine. Today, this version of God enjoys between 1.5 and 2 billion followers. He also split into a trinity consisting of God, his human Son, and the less well-defined Holy Spirit.

The main architects of this new religion would be a young preacher, a healer born in Nazareth, an apostle who came after him, and the Roman Church. The new god and his religion would be further defined and shaped throughout the next two thousand years.

The making of He who became known as the Christian God began with the emergence of Jewish preachers during the Roman occupation of Judea (Israel). As with the transformations wrought by Moses, the Christian God was not new; indeed, He was directly adapted from the Jewish God.

One of these new Jewish preachers was named Jesus.

A Jewish Preacher, and the Transformation of the Hebrew God

To understand the transformation of a breakaway Jewish sect into Christianity, we must first examine the political and religious landscape in which Jesus (later called The Christ, a Greek term meaning Anointed One) was born. In 3 BCE, Judea was under Roman occupation, with a well-trained legion of soldiers present to ensure the interests of the Roman Empire. Herod the Great, appointed by the Romans as the King of the Jews, nominally ruled Judea. In turn Pontius Pilate was the appointed Roman prefect (administrator) during the preaching career of Jesus. Under the Roman system, most political control was left to local populations, as long as their leaders respected Roman rule and paid tribute regularly. Much of the political power was in the hands of the Jewish High Priests.

The local religious population then consisted of both Jews and gentiles. The Jews believed in the God of Moses, while the non-Jews believed in a variety of pagan gods (including the gods of Greece and Rome), magic, and superstition. The Jewish religion centered around a temple, served by priests making sacrifices to Yahweh (God). The Priests, as ordered by God in the Old Testament, were descendants from Aaron of the tribe Levi. At the time, the Jewish religion was under threat of the infusion of Greco-Roman (Hellenistic) religious beliefs and gods. The Jews were the Chosen Race of their God, but lately, it seemed that God was forsaking them. Politically and religiously, the Jews were under attack from Hellenistic culture and religion.

Further weakening the Jewish religion were the different belief systems that had developed within Judaism itself. Judaism was split into three primary groups. The Sadducee party consisted of the priests who controlled the temple, with many of them enjoying a privileged life. The Essenes were a mystical-religious movement with their own interpretation of the Jewish faith. The Pharisees were another, and they in particular were making significant headway in transforming Judaism. Most importantly for the rise of Christianity, the Pharisees introduced the belief of resurrection after death, which had previously been a concept foreign to Judaism.

Tension between the Jewish religious groups and their occupiers was at an all-time high. Any dissent or sign of an uprising was quickly suppressed by the Romans. The suppression of the Jews reawakened the ancient Jewish dream of a Messiah, send by God, to free them and give them back their political determination. Within these times of turmoil and uncertainty, Jesus of Nazareth was born.

The Birth of Jesus

According to the Bible, Jesus was born in a stable while his parents were traveling. Rather than taking place in late December, it seems likely that the event actually occurred in September, during an annual pilgrimage to Bethlehem. This belief in a humble beginning set the tone for a new ideology, wherein (ideally) poverty and class were of little importance. Only spiritual richness mattered.

Unsurprisingly, the birth of Jesus was soon shrouded in legend. As far as we can tell, the mother of Jesus, Mary, was engaged to Joseph, but became pregnant out of wedlock. Pregnancy out of wedlock earned a woman death or exile in the Jewish community. According to the Bible, however, the Angel Gabriel appeared to Joseph, explaining that this was the child of God, and to call him Jesus.

Jesus, as Son of both God and Man, became central to the religion that grew up around him. This belief was not uncommon to earlier religious; demigods—half-man, half-god—often served as messengers and representatives between the heavenly and human worlds. Several ancient folklores and beliefs contain the tale of a woman giving virgin birth to the child of a god. In Greek mythology, for example, Perseus was the child of Danae, who was impregnated by Zeus.

Demigods typically have special qualities, and can move between the world of the living and the dead. They are also superior in many ways to normal people. Most Egyptian pharaohs also claimed to be of divine descent, with human mothers and godly fathers. In the Hindu belief system, virgin births are also common. Karna, the great warrior of ancient India, was the son of the woman Kunti and the god Surya. His mother also retained her virginity.

The belief in Jesus as the Son of God was crystallized in 325 AD, nearly 300 years after his lifetime. At that time, the Roman Church received orders from the Roman Emperor Constantine and his council to determine that Jesus had, in fact, been conceived as the Son of God in a virgin birth.

The Making of Jesus

Little information is available about the life of Jesus from a point just after his birth until he started preaching. Even his preaching career was short, lasting only 1-2 years. The only real information we have regarding his life is in the books of Matthew and Luke in the Bible, which were written 40-100 years after his death. Unfortunately, they conflict; for example, though both track his lineage back to the great Jewish king, David, the lineages reported are different.

Roman and other documents of the era contain no references to Jesus, requiring us to theorize or hypothesize about his childhood years. What turns a humble boy, supposedly born in a stable, into one of the most influential figures in history? The teachings ascribed to him still reverberate through today's churches, which boast more than 2 billion followers by some counts. Was he indeed the Son of God, or was he turned into the Son of God by those who came after him? We do not have a single word written down by him; only hearsay recorded decades after his death. Some of those writings are so controversial that they have never been accepted as part of the "official" Christian Bible. Even those writings accepted by the Roman Catholic Church originate from many different sources, with many internal inconsistencies. The Bible is more of an anthology than a single, unified work.

We know that Jesus had brothers and sisters, and it's easy to assume that he must have had a very normal childhood for those times: processing through the developmental phases from infant to toddler; quarrelling with his siblings; playing at home and outdoors. We know Jesus was a Jew, and that his people were oppressed under Roman rule. The anguish of his people, their ideas, and their religious beliefs must have been formative in his childhood. We have one reference in the Bible in which, at age 12, Jesus deserted his parents. Only after three days had passed did they find him at the local temple, sitting with the teachers and arguing with them. It seems from this that even from a young age, Jesus already had a keen interest in religion. He was probably extraordinarily gifted, and must have formed his own religious thoughts, framework, and answers early on. Was Jesus already considering priesthood by age 12?

Whatever the case, the time was ripe for change when Jesus began his ministry. There were many other emerging Jewish preachers at around the same time, though most were apocalypse preachers, forecasting the end of the world upon the coming of a Messiah to free the Jewish nation. Faith healers were also common, "curing" people in the name of God.

The Jewish Preachers

One of the foremost preachers Jesus' time was John the Baptist. According to the Bible he lived in the wild on locusts and wild honey, clothed in camel's hair with a leather belt around his waist. He preached an end of the world message that would restore Israel and God; his message emphasized that one should repent now, as the Kingdom of God was coming. Indeed, he was preaching the ancient dream of Judaism that was established in the time of Moses. It was said that John the Baptist attracted large crowds, and used baptism— a symbolic immersion in water—as a symbol to cleanse one of sin and thus obtain the grace of God. This ritual is very much part of Christianity today, but it did not begin with Christianity. The use of water to ritually cleanse oneself is a common theme in many religions, including modern Hinduism.

John taught that to be saved and find the grace of God, you needed to be baptized—even if you were born a Jew. His ministry was brutally ended; he was imprisoned and later executed by Herod, as he was becoming a political threat to the Jewish King's rule. However, his preaching and impact remain alive today, and not only in the Christian church. Today there is still a group in Iraq, the Mandaeans, that believes in John the Baptist as the last messiah.

Another prominent preacher of the times was Judas of Galilee. He started a fourth sect of Judaism, with God alone as the ruler of Judea.

His revolt was brutally suppressed by the Romans. Another Jewish preacher, Theudas, also started his own sect within Judaism. Flavius Josephus, born just a few years after the death of Jesus, describes Theudas in his book *The Antiquities of the Jews* (published 1737) thus:

> Now it came to pass, while Fadus was procurator of Judea, that a certain magician, whose name was Theudas, persuaded a great part of the people to take their effects with them, and follow him to the river Jordan; for he told them he was a prophet, and that he would, by his own command, divide the river, and afford them an easy passage over it; and many were deluded by his words. However, Fadus did not permit them to make any advantage of his wild attempt, but sent a troop of horsemen out against them; who, falling upon them unexpectedly, slew many of them, and took many of them alive. They also took Theudas alive, and cut off his head, and carried it to Jerusalem."

The time of Jesus was clearly an era of Jewish struggle for political freedom. It was also an era during which Judaism was under severe strain, when reform was needed. The political and religious pressure of the times triggered the emergence of many Jewish prophets who opposed Roman rule, believing that God would lead them to victory, that the end of the world was near, and that the Kingdom of God was fast approaching. The Jewish nation was desperately seeking for a Messiah—specifically a military leader—sent by their God to release them from Roman rule.

It is difficult to say whether Jesus was influenced by John the Baptist; certainly they knew each other, and the Bible also tells us that John baptized Jesus. Jesus may have been his cousin, and may have studied under John the Baptist for a time. In the beginning, Jesus himself was an apocalypse prophet preaching the end of the world, like so many of his fellows. He foresaw an end of days when all nations would clash, and the sun would be darkened—a time when the sign of the Son of Man would appear in the heavens, and angels would congregate to gather the Elect.

A New Sect within Judaism

Jesus' preaching was to the Jews alone, and it wasn't long before he started building a large following. He began attacking the existing Jewish priesthood, which had become a privileged class within Jewish society that did not hesitate to wield their power even in the religion's holy places. Indeed, the Jewish temples became places where many people plied their trades, and those in control of those temples used them to gain resources and power. Jesus soon started an uprising among the Jewish priesthood.

1. Then spoke Jesus to the multitude, and to his disciples,

6. They love the uppermost (best) rooms at feasts, and the chief seats in the synagogues,

7. And greetings in the markets, and to be called of men, Rabbi, Rabbi.

Jesus called the scribes and Pharisees hypocrites, and accused them of being like white tombs: appearing beautiful outside, but inside being full of dead men's bones and uncleanliness. Jesus was preaching a new social order and reform in Judaism—an order where being poor and ordinary made no difference. All were equal in the eyes of God, he taught; wealth was of no significance, and the poor would one day take their rightful place among the Elect. Jesus ate with the despised, the tax collectors, and the sinners. He taught that salvation was all about the individual, via their actions and thoughts. He attacked the strict class hierarchy of the Jewish religious leaders, asking, "What makes you, as a rich man, better than a poor man with a noble mind and good heart?"

Jesus preached:

20 ...Blessed be ye poor: for yours is the Kingdom of God.

21 Blessed are ye that hunger now: for ye shall be filled. Blessed are ye that weep now: for ye shall laugh.

Jesus and/or the group of prophets he belonged to advocated the following ideals:

1. It is not the material world but Heaven that is important;

2. Forgive those that hate you and turn the other cheek;

3. You will be resurrected from death if you believe;

4. The end of the world is near, so repent your sins now;

5. God will come to judge, and evil will be forever banished by the good;

6. This world is temporary; your life should be lived to gain access to the afterlife;

7. Status and wealth does not matter, but your heart and loyalty to God does.

The teachings of Jesus also included preaching the existing Jewish laws—teachings that are still a cause of much bewilderment and confusion today. It's uncertain whether some of these strictures were actually taught by Jesus, or added to his canon by clergy after his death. For example:

And *I say unto you, Whosoever divorces his wife, except it be for fornication, and shall marry another, commits adultery: and whoso marries her which is put away also commits adultery.*

Jesus was also a faith healer, and according to the Bible, produced distinct miracles. He was able to cure the sick, including raising people from death; exorcise demons from a person; and rule over nature. The New Testament contains several accounts of miraculous healings attributed to Jesus.

1. And he entered into a ship, and passed over, and came into his own city.

2. And, behold, they brought to him a man sick of the palsy, lying on a bed: and Jesus, seeing their faith, said unto the sick of the palsy; Son, be of good cheer; thy sins be forgiven thee.

3. And, behold, certain of the scribes said within themselves, This man blasphemeth.

4. And Jesus, knowing their thoughts, said, Wherefore think ye evil in your hearts?

5. For whether it is easier, to say, Thy sins be forgiven thee; or to say, Arise, and walk?

6. But that ye may know that the Son of Man hath power on earth to forgive sins, (then saith he to the sick of the palsy,) Arise, take up thy bed, and go unto thine house.

7. And he arose, and departed to his house.

8. But when the multitudes saw it, they marveled, and glorified God, which had given such power unto men.

Here is an example of Jesus exorcising a demon:

26 And he said to them, Why are you fearful, O ye of little faith? Then he arose, and rebuked the winds and the sea; and there was a great calm.

27 But the men marveled, saying, What manner of man is this, that even the winds and the sea obey him!

28 And when he was come to the other side into the country of the Gergesenes, there met him two possessed with devils, coming out of the tombs, exceeding fierce, so that no man might pass by that way.

29 And, behold, they cried out, saying, What have we to do with thee, Jesus, thou Son of God? Art thou come hither to torment us before the time?

30 And there was a good way off from them an herd of many swine feeding.

31 So the devils besought him, saying, If thou cast us out, suffer us to go away into the herd of swine.

32 And he said unto them, Go. And when they were come out, they went into the herd of swine: and, behold, the whole herd of swine ran violently down a steep place into the sea, and perished in the waters.

Jesus was not only a preacher, but also a healer. Did this power come from God, or was Jesus able to deceive his audience into believing in his healings? In his time, miracle workers were common. We know that Jesus said that he was unable to perform miracles in Nazareth, his birth town, as they did not believe in him there. In those ancient days, the use of the scientific method to prove or disprove phenomenon did not exist. The truth is, even today faith healers are not uncommon, especially in 'primitive' tribes; for example, thousands of people in the traditional Zulu culture of South Africa will happily swear upon the healing capabilities of a Sangoma. Most ancient tribes had faith healers of their own.

In Jesus's era, there was a strong belief in supernatural curing. The Pool of Bethesda, for example, was seen as a place where the ill could be cured. Those in the pool would wait for an angel to stir the water to heal them. Exorcism of invading spirits was also common, and is still in practice today, with some churches employing official exorcists. Indeed, exorcism is abundant in man's religious journey. We find exorcism even in the Native American tribes, where medicine men often expelled invading spirits to heal a patient. Egyptian priests often cast out bad spirits as well.

With the advent of modern science, we now know that most (if not all) of the so-called "possession" phenomena arose from mental illnesses or other brain dysfunctions. These include epilepsy, schizophrenia, dissociative identity disorder, and a host of others. Their origins are to be found in the psychology of the individual, and the function and chemical balance in their brains.

Today we have the knowledge necessary to diagnose and treat these disorders. However, in the Biblical era a child having an epileptic attack, or a person with schizophrenia, was seen as being possessed by demons or bad spirits. Most of these poor souls were probably murdered as a result. While some of the more religious among us still believe in possession, modern science has yet to record a single *prima-facie* case of demonic possession; so it is without hesitation that we can reject the exorcisms performed by Jesus. The persons "exorcized" by Jesus had mental illnesses, nothing more. At the most, one can accept that perhaps the afflicted might have believed so fervently in Jesus' healing powers that the symptoms of the mental illness disappeared after he "exorcised" them, in a sort of placebo effect. But in cases such as these, the mental illness is suppressed only temporarily.

The Jewish community then and today has never accepted the miracles of Jesus as such.

As an apocalypse prophet, Jesus triggered an uprising against the established Jewish priesthood, introducing what he considered a better social order. He travelled Judea delivering sermons, and possibly baptizing people as taught by John the Baptist. He was a faith healer and exorcist. But it was his resistance to and attack upon the Jewish religious establishment that would lead to his death. They had to kill him to retain their power, and Jesus was no fool; he had to have known this.

The Death of Jesus

Jesus must have become more and more convinced of his own teachings and the need to reform the Jewish religion. His uprising and resistance came to a head during the Passover feast that most Jews attended every year in Jerusalem—an event that was closely monitored by the Romans, as the festival attracted thousands of Jews and had a history of resistance. Jesus rode into Jerusalem on a donkey, supported by his followers, who lined the path with clothes and branches: the reformer and preacher to the masses and poor, entering the hub and core of the Jewish religious establishment.

Jesus intended to strike at the very heart of the Judaism. He went immediately to the Jewish Temple, overturned the tables of the money-changers and the merchants set up there, and started preaching his own beliefs: a direct challenge to the Jewish priests. The established priesthood was threatened by his confrontation, but dared not try to eject or kill him, given his large following. They challenged him with all kinds of questions, hoping to find a reason to arrest him, but Jesus skillfully provided answers to these and their further allegations.

The counsel of priests finally ordered the arrest of Jesus on a charge of blasphemy. As they did not have the authority of execution under Roman rule, they took him to Pontius Pilate the Roman prefect, where they charged Jesus with disturbing the public peace and opposing the paying of taxes. Pilate immediately recognized this as a Jewish matter, a political move by the prevailing priests and religious establishment to silence Jesus.

But Pilate was also responsible from keeping the masses under control. After trying vainly to grant Jesus a reprieve, he gave in to the Jewish priests and ordered Jesus crucified. The crucifixion of Jesus was immortalized as the founding event of Christianity. The revolutionary, the reformer, the one who wanted to change the social order, was to be killed in the most inhuman way possible. Humiliated, he was taken to prison and taunted before being taken to his place of execution, dragging the means of his own death—a crude wooden crucifix—behind him. Nailed to the cross, he was raised up to die a slow and agonizing death. His pain and suffering must have been unbearable.

The death of Jesus left his followers and disciples in mourning, without a leader. His uprising and execution during the Passover feast, that gathering of thousands of Jews, must have reverberated through Judea; and it has certainly reverberated down through history. The jealous overreaction of the Jewish priests who ordered his destruction seeded his ideas even more solidly in the psyches of his followers, and drew in even more followers. The revolution had started; his martyrdom gave birth to an entirely new religion and world order—despite the fact that most of his teachings were transmitted orally and remained unrecorded for decades, until the first were written down about 40 years later.

Many of these writings have never been accepted as authentic, while others have been through numerous language translations and have been heavily edited. We will most probably never know the original teachings of Jesus, or how accurate the accepted Gospels we know today are. Those who came after him, most notably Paul and the Roman Church, would define his teachings for him, creating an entirely new religion out of Judaism. This new religion, Christianity, was a religion not for Jews, but for the specific followers of Jesus as the Messiah, the Christ.

Even today, Judaism does not acknowledge Jesus or his divinity.

The death of Jesus became shrouded in the mystical. A new legend was born: a legend of the resurrection of Jesus after his death, which became another cornerstone of Christianity. With the death of Jesus most of his disciples fled, fearing for their lives. But one, a woman, was brave enough to stay with him: Maria Magdalene. Grief-stricken, she witnessed his crucifixion. Three days after his body was laid down in a tomb and sealed with a boulder, Maria Magdalene went to visit his tomb.

On her arrival she found the boulder rolled away; inside were only the remnants of his clothing. Did the Roman soldiers or the Jewish priests remove the body of Jesus to make sure Jesus did not become a martyr, or did some of his followers do so in order to give him a proper burial at another location? Whatever the case, the event assured he would not be forgotten, cementing his martyrdom as a central tenet of the new religion.

The grief of Maria Magdalene was unbearable, and in her anguish she "saw" an angel sitting at the tomb. Jesus also appeared to some of his disciples, who at first did not recognize him; only later did they realize it was Jesus. We will most probably never know the truth about what happened to the body of Jesus after his death, but whatever occurred, it was assumed that Jesus was brought back to life before he ascended to Heaven to take his rightful place next to God. Resurrection, therefore, is the foundation of the Christian faith.

A Closer Look at Rebirth

The concept of resurrection existed long before the ministry of Jesus, with some Jewish sects borrowing the new belief from older religions. James H. Charlesworth (2008) points out that the two most likely sources of the Jewish resurrection beliefs are Ugarit and the Zoroastrianism movement in Iran. Ugarit (today Ras Shamra) in Syria was an ancient port city that most probably arose about 6,000 BCE and reached its political height from 1,450-1,200 BCE.

The city was long lost, but in 1928 CE, a peasant accidentally hit an old tomb as he ploughed a field. Later excavations revealed a large, important city with a well-developed infrastructure, including two libraries. Hundreds of clay tablets were found there, documenting the myths and beliefs of these people. Studying the religion of the Ugarites, we find a belief in both immortality and resurrection. It also gives us useful insight into and detailed descriptions of the Canaanite beliefs before the Jewish tribes settled in the same region. It's almost certain that these beliefs had a major influence on the developing Jewish religion, which adopted some of the central Ugarit tenets.

Even more compelling evidence comes from the Zoroastrian movement, which started 800 BCE and lasted well into the 8th century CE as one of the Middle East's largest religions. It still has somewhere between 145,000 and 210,000 adherents worldwide. This religion and its guiding philosophies were founded by the prophet Zoroaster, who lived about 800 BCE; it's based on the worship of Ahura Mazda, a supreme god and creator of all, similar to the Jewish God. It has been said that this religion has had more influence on humankind, directly or indirectly, than any other faith (Boyce, 2001). The central tenets of Zoroastrianism are:

1. There is one universal god, Ahura Mazda, both in this world and beyond;
2. This god is the antithesis of chaos and evil, and is involved in a universal conflict wherein humanity has an active role and participation;
3. Good acts, words, and deeds are required to maintain happiness and keep evil at bay. Active participation is required;
4. At the end of time, a savior will appear to bring about a final revolution;
5. Ultimately, there will be an end to evil through a battle between the forces of good and evil;
6. Ahura Mazda will ultimately prevail over evil, and the world will end at this point;
7. In the end everyone, including the dead, will be reunited in life.

After the victory of good, everyone who has ever lived will be resurrected in a spiritual body and soul. The sick and suffering of all ages will return as healthy adults. Their spiritual bodies will not need food, and conflict and evil will not exist. Nor will these bodies cast any shadows. All humans will have one language, without any cultural boundaries; we will all be one, all of us immortal, happy, and enjoying the glory of Ahura Mazda under his patronage.

It is almost certain that the Jews borrowed this belief of resurrection from the Zoroastrians, because resurrection did not feature in Judaism until their contact with the Persian culture and belief systems. There is also very little in the Hebrew Bible pointing toward resurrection.

By the time of Jesus, resurrection had taken root and flourished in the Jewish religion. It had already influenced one of the main three "streams" of Judaism, the Pharisees. Jesus himself was a Pharisee, and as such preached the promise of universal resurrection after the end of the world, when evil would finally be destroyed. The resurrection concept was enjoying much greater acceptance in Jesus's day, as it provided an escape or solution to the injustice, suppression, and cruelty the Jews then suffered under the Romans and others. If they could not experience comfort and joy in this life, then they could at least look forward to a time when the righteous would be blessed with eternal life and justice, the bad banished forever. According to this promise, God would rule the world after Resurrection, and the Jews would have their political Kingdom back.

The resurrection concept then further evolved, such that only those that believed in a specific religion or god would be able to get into this afterlife. This was possibly introduced as a way to exclude the Romans and non-Jews from the hereafter. The same concept of resurrection also found its way in Islam, introduced by Muhammad, probably drawn from his contact with the Jewish and Christian beliefs. Nowadays resurrection has become exclusive—an unfortunate development, as both Christianity and Islam claim that only those believing in their particular gods have any right to the afterlife.

So who was Jesus, really? By all accounts he was a Jewish prophet who propagated reform in Judaism. He preached a classless society where the individual (not his status) would determine his value and acceptance by God. He introduced a new belief system in Judaism, one opposed to established Jewish thought. Through his preaching and apparent healings he built a huge following in Judea. In the end, he suffered a cruel death for his resistance and reforms. He was a prophet who might have remained largely unknown, if he had not been martyred by his enemies in so drastic a fashion that his followers constructed an entire belief system around him.

Christianity, as we will see, was not so much the product of Jesus but rather the product of those who came after him, preaching in his name. The main architects of early Christianity after Jesus were the Apostle Paul and the Roman Catholic Church.

Paul as the Architect of Christianity

After the death of Jesus, his disciples dispersed, many fleeing for their lives or returning to their previous lives. Their Messiah and leader were dead. In the absence of his leadership, the new movement was in danger of dying out and disappearing. Just two of his disciples, namely Peter and James, continued his preaching and teachings. As Jesus had not written anything down, his teachings must have been passed on as *they* perceived the new doctrine, shaped by their years with Jesus and the ideas he conveyed to them. They were orally transmitting the message of Jesus; how closely their renditions resembled the original is impossible to tell.

Ultimately, another person was to shape Jesus's ideas into the new religion that became Christianity. Many authors after him added to this doctrine, which was then further developed by the organized Roman Catholic Church until it crystallized into today's Christianity. This person never met Jesus; in fact, he did not start preaching until about 35 years after Jesus died. Being educated formally and also possessing Roman citizenship, this influential individual laid a firm foundation for modern Christianity by formally documenting its central tenets and beliefs.

In truth, it's likely that more than one person shaped this new Jesus-centered religion by building on his crucifixion, purported resurrection, and by immortalizing him as the Son of God. But no one did more to shape proto-Christianity than the Apostle Paul. He preached to the Jews and gentiles (non-Jews) alike, transforming this new religion for the gentiles; Jesus himself preached only to the Jews. Thirteen of the 27 books of the New Testament are attributed to Paul, and another book (Acts) was written about Paul by a companion; those 14 books comprise more than half of the New Testament.

Judaism for Non-Jews

As previously outlined, Jesus and his new movement had threatened the ancient Jewish religion, and were seen as blasphemous by the Pharisee and Sadducee Jews alike. The movement was revolutionary in its efforts to reform the ancient beliefs and practices, which Jesus perceived as outdated and, in many cases, corrupt and/or damaging to the Jewish people. His death temporary removed the threat, but his martyrdom ensured that some of his followers would still preach his message—and that some of their followers would later take up the mantle as well.

No one fanned the flame more than Paul—more or less a Hellenistic Jew, who had already assimilated much from the Greek culture into his belief system, as opposed to the more orthodox Jews. Paul came from the city of Tarsus, which was then an intellectual center. In essence, we have a person who already doubted Orthodox Judaism, was heavily influenced by the Greek culture, and was exposed to an intellectual environment that challenged the normal and the accepted.

In the beginning, Paul was a fervent follower of the Pharisee sect of Judaism—and, ironically, harassed and persecuted the disciples of Jesus in and around Jerusalem. But one incident (or alleged incident) was to have a profound impact on Paul. As told in the New Testament, Paul had a spiritual revelation on his way to Damascus. Jesus himself appeared to Paul, accompanied by a bright light that partially blinded Paul for three days, and demanded to know why he was persecuting the Christians.

After this experience, Paul rejected his previous beliefs and adopted the reforms of the new Christian movement.

This was a momentous event in history, as Paul would soon set out to develop and compose the initial Christian doctrine. But what was this revelation and blinding light that changed his beliefs? It's hard to say, but Paul must have come into increasing contact with the followers of the new movement as he persecuted them. With exposure to the new doctrine, he must have started questioning his own belief system. He was also well versed in Roman reasoning and the Roman development of law.

It's quite likely that Paul experienced an inner struggle between his original beliefs and convictions and the tenets of the new Jesus movement. In his misery and doubt, he finally succumbed to his own reasoning and accepted the new belief system, replacing his previous belief system with the new one. The intense emotional high he experienced was like a brilliant light that left him in a daze. During this period, Paul started constructing his new belief based on the teaching of the new Jewish prophets and Jesus—a new belief which would ultimately culminate in Christianity, to form the basis of the New Testament that, when joined with the ancient Jewish Torah, would result in the Holy Bible.

Paul's most significant contribution was his decision to bring the new religion to the gentiles; because until then, the teachings of Jesus were still reserved for Jews, which limited their wider acceptance. To take on the beliefs of Jesus, one had to convert to Judaism; and at the time, not being a member of the Jewish race made this very difficult. Paul, himself a Jew, must have reasoned that the God of Jesus was also valid for others. Paul struck a deal with Peter, one of Jesus's direct disciples, that Peter would continue preaching for the Jews while Paul targeted the gentiles or non-Jews.

At this stage there were still conditions that a non-Jew had to meet before he was allowed to become part of the new movement, including that males had to be circumcised. With time Paul would also remove these constraints, to enable him to bring the new religion to the masses. But more than simply teach the words of Jesus, Paul also helped turn Jesus into a martyr and promoted him as the Son of God. Jesus himself never claimed to be the Son of God; Paul and those after him invented that claim as part of their effort to construct Christianity with Jesus as its central figure.

To accept Christianity, one has to accept the divinity of Jesus, his crucifixion as a sacrifice for the sins of all mankind, and take him on as one's Savior. Let me re-emphasize: *Jesus never preached these beliefs.* Those who came after him constructed Christianity.

Dominant in this new religion was also the involvement of Jesus in the coming apocalypse, and the resurrection of those believing in God. The religion of Paul, with Jesus as its central figure, preached the following:

- Jesus lives in Heaven and was the Messiah;
- Jesus is the Son of God;
- Jesus will return soon, defeat all the dark forces, and liberate the world forever from sin and evil;
- The non-Jews who believe in Jesus and the Jewish god will also be saved;
- Death is not the end, but the start of eternal life for those who believe;
- Jesus died for our sins, and thereby freed believers from sin and guilt.

A New Religion is Created

We can outline the development of Christianity as follows:

1. A new reform movement evolved in Judaism, led by prophets such as John the Baptist and Jesus, that had the apocalypse and resurrection as central themes;
2. The death of Jesus, which turned him into a martyr;
3. Paul and those after him, elevating Jesus to a figure with God-like qualities;
4. A new religion developed with Jesus as the Son of God as its central theme, interwoven with Judaic belief systems.

As a Roman citizen, the Apostle Paul travelled all over the Roman world, visiting synagogues for a few days before moving on. He preached to the non-Jews (the gentiles) in the marketplaces and wherever he could find a sympathetic audience. His preaching was not without controversy, and the conflict between Judaism and the new Jesus movement continued.

> *42 And when the Jews were gone out of the synagogue, the Gentiles besought that these words might be preached to them the next sabbath.*
>
> *43 Now when the congregation was broken up, many of the Jews and religious proselytes followed Paul and Barnabas: who, speaking to them, persuaded them to continue in the grace of God.*
>
> *44 And the next sabbath day came almost the whole city together to hear the word of God.*
>
> *45 But when the Jews saw the multitudes, they were filled with envy, and spoke against those things which were spoken by Paul, contradicting and blaspheming.*
>
> *46 Then Paul and Barnabas waxed bold, and said, It was necessary that the word of God should first have been spoken to you: but seeing ye put it from you, and judge yourselves unworthy of everlasting life, lo, we turn to the Gentiles.*
>
> *47 For so had the Lord commanded us, saying, I have set thee to be a light of the Gentiles, that thou should be for salvation unto the ends of the earth.*
>
> *48 And when the Gentiles heard this, they were glad, and glorified the word of the Lord: and as many as were ordained to eternal life believed.*
>
> *49 And the word of the Lord was published throughout all the region.*

In the places he visited, Paul would preach and then also set up a small group (sect kernel) to keep advocating his beliefs. The times were ripe for a new message. The changes brought by the new Jewish prophets and Jesus had already infiltrated the general population and Jewish community alike. Paul organized and advanced the movement started by Jesus as he went. The kernel groups he left behind would recruit more people until they grew big enough to become churches, often even constructing or converting a building to be their place of worship.

The established Jewish priesthood must have watched in horror as this new sect started taking root.

Travel was arduous and slow in the time of Paul, and he could at most visit these sects that he left behind only once every few years; and sometimes he never returned again. He used some of his assistants, such as Timothy and Titus, to every now and then go back to these early churches to strengthen them and preach the message further. Others also started preaching and spreading the new message. The new movement was slowly taking hold.

Paul's greatest legacy, however, was the letters that he wrote to these early churches, codifying the beliefs of the new movement. Some of these churches or sect groups had begun promulgating their own doctrines or falling back on old beliefs. Paul would then write them a long letter to explain his message. It is these letters that now comprise most of the New Testament—human letters that contain Paul's own ideas and perceptions that are now believed to be the Word of God and, as such, are followed by 2 billion Christians the world over. These letters also exude the conservatism of Paul, which is still influencing our ultra-modern world today. As women then had inferior status in society, it is no surprise that Paul's letters contain many references to women:

2 For the woman which has a husband is bound by the law to her husband so long as he lives; but if the husband be dead, she is loosed from the law of her husband.

3 So then if, while her husband is alive, she be married to another man, she shall be called an adulteress: but if her husband be dead, she is free from that law; so that she is no adulteress, though she is married to another man.

From Corinthians (a letter to the Christians at Corinth, Greece), Paul stated:

11.9 Neither was the man created for the woman; but the woman for the man.

14.34 Let your women keep silence in the churches: for it is not permitted unto them to speak; but they are commanded to be under obedience as also said the law.

14.35 And if they will learn anything let them ask their husbands at home: for it is a shame for women to speak in the church.

Paul also advocated a conservative approach to sexuality, most probably originating from his conservative upbringing in Judaism. Judaism then prescribed an expected sexual behavior, with many prohibitions on sexual practices. These included homosexuality, sexual activity before marriage, sexual immorality, and more. The sexual standpoint of Paul still has a profound bearing on today's world. His teachings forced women to wear hot, long clothing covering most of their bodies for centuries, and sex was seen as necessary but distasteful, a shameful act never to be spoken of in public. Most state and local governments in the United States still consider homosexuality a crime. Paul wrote in his letters:

27 And likewise also the men, leaving the natural use of the woman, burned in their lust one toward another; men with men working that which is unseemly, and receiving in themselves error.

Another influence of Paul on the Christian world was his high esteem for celibacy.

1 Now concerning the things whereof ye wrote unto me: It is good for a man not to touch a woman.

Paul believed that by following celibacy, one could devote oneself completely to God. As such, we have nuns and priests today who are not allowed to have sexual relations, and are perceived as having a higher morality because they have conquered their sexual desires in order to focus on their worship of God. Married Christians lie a tier lower, as they have succumbed to sexual relations. This view on the part of Paul may have derived from his own lack of sexual drive or from strong personal convictions about sexuality—and it was to mold Christianity for thousands of years to come.

Paul also wrote that one should honor and be obedient to authority.

1 Let every soul be subject unto the higher powers. For there is no power but of God: the powers that be are ordained of God.
2 Whosoever therefore resist the power, resist the ordinance of God: and they that resist shall receive to themselves damnation.

This statement was used to justify the divine authority of the Church, regardless of whether or not its decisions or actions were wrong or unjust. Later Christian churches used this authority to plunge the world into centuries of darkness, with little development or creativity. In Christianity, you are not allowed to resist or question those in divine power.

Using Sin to Advance Christianity

Paul or/and those after him also introduced the concept of the sin of mankind, originating from the Jewish myth of Adam and Eve. All humans are sinful, they taught, even from birth; and this Original Sin derived from the error of Adam and Eve in challenging God. Thus, God punished not just them but also their descendants; that is, all of humanity, from the highest to the lowest. Christianity teaches that only by taking Jesus unconditionally as your savior can you absolve yourself from sin, and be rescued from destruction. One must genuinely believe that Jesus allowed himself to be sacrificed in order to take your sin upon himself, so that you may be forgiven in the eyes of God.

Paul's doctrine still causes untold agony today throughout the world, as those steeped in the Christian beliefs are in daily conflict not to sin, and to keep asking for mercy and forgiveness from Jesus. This notion is installed in young children almost from birth.

Like Jesus, Paul continually upset the Jewish establishment with his teachings. In one particular incident, he caused so much anger in the Jewish community that they pulled him out of a synagogue and handed him over to a Roman captain to be executed. Being a Roman citizen and thus protected by Roman law, however, Paul was able to escape the wrath of the crowds by calling for a fair trial. He appealed directly to the Caesar for a trial in Rome; and so, he was transported there, a very long journey.

We have no information about what happened to Paul after he arrived in Rome; either he was executed by the Romans, or disappeared into obscurity. In either case, the architect of one of today's largest, most influential religions was essentially dead. His message and ideas, however, would live on in the sects he left behind, which gained momentum in the years after his disappearance. His letters to these early churches became the cornerstone of Christianity.

Paul was the greatest architect of Christianity, much more so than Jesus.

Other Architects of Christianity

But Paul and Jesus were not the only architects of the new movement in Judaism. Its origins can be traced to John the Baptist and the other revolutionary Jewish preachers who preceded Jesus and were his contemporaries. The disciples of Jesus also had a major influence in the shaping of the new movement, with Peter and James continuing his teachings. Countless more would add their ideas and thoughts to the new doctrine in the next few centuries. Those with the greatest influence were probably those who, in later years, documented the new belief system. Writings that contained some of the original beliefs of Jesus intermingled with the interpretation and understanding of various authors. A host of writings appeared in the first few centuries after Jesus, with many "scriptures" far removed from each other in terms of narrative and their understanding of Jesus. Only later would the Roman Church select specific scriptures as valid, which were then assembled into the Bible as the confirmed Word of God.

It would be wrong to assume that Christianity has become monolithic, however. Christianity has in fact become very complex, with thousands of different churches, many sects, and different teachings and beliefs propounded by the many Christian denominations. This religion is still very much still in flux and development.

Of course, the Roman Catholic Church also played an enormous role in shaping modern Christianity; so let's take a look at the Catholic Church, and how Christianity developed after the death of Jesus.

When the disciples of Jesus and his other contemporaries and acquaintances began passing away, they left a kind of power vacuum, with no central authority or policy-making body left to shape and monitor their new belief system. Oral tradition was used to pass along the acts and words of Jesus. Only after the destruction of the Second Temple of the Jews were the first chapters of the New Testament written down, with more writings added to the canon up until the 3rd century CE.

The beliefs of the first Christians were in direct opposition to the rule of Rome and its official pagan religion, so Christianity also served as a resistance movement against the Roman Empire, attracting more and more people. The Christians believed their God to be the supreme god, with higher authority than the Roman Emperor. Persecution of the Christians was common at first, with many of those following the teachings of Jesus leading secret lives. After the great fire of AD 64, when much of Rome was destroyed, the Roman emperor Nero accused the Christians of causing the blaze. As a result, they were persecuted even further. Christianity remained an underground religion for centuries, resisting the authority of Roman rule even within Rome itself. The excellent road infrastructure and relative safety it brought travelers via the Pax Romana helped spread the Christian message across the Roman Empire.

In 313, the adoption of Christianity by the Roman Emperor Constantine changed the fortunes of Christianity profoundly. Constantine was the son of an army officer and his lesser wife or concubine Helena. His father rose to the rank of Deputy Emperor, and soon left Helena and his son to marry another woman for political reasons. There is some evidence that Helena was a Christian, and conveyed the Christian religion to Constantine. His mother must have had great aspirations for her son; and like so many mothers in similar circumstances, fostered the idea and hope of her son taking his rightful place at the reins of power.

Eventually, Constantine *did* become the leader of the mighty Roman Empire. After winning the important battle of the Milvian Bride, he announced that the Christian God had led him to victory; and by doing so, legitimized the Christian faith. He also supported the Church financially and appointed Christians to important positions in his government; and soon Christianity was accepted throughout the Empire.

Indeed, it wasn't long before Christianity became the state religion, with the Emperor its most fervent follower. Other belief systems were shunted aside and in many cases deemed blasphemous. One soon needed Christian credentials to be appointed to higher positions and find favor with the Emperor, so many converted for these reasons. Major creeds, decisions, and interpretations of Jesus' message were made at the time of Constantine. This was the era during which most of Christianity's beliefs were codified, laying the groundwork for the system still followed today.

Soon all of Europe was gripped by the ideology of Christianity, which (in part) resulted in centuries of stagnation of thought and creativity. The new belief system was to influence government policy at the fundamental level; and soon the church *became* government, with reason often replaced with religious ideology. Only in the 17th and 18th centuries would a wave of liberation wash over Europe, somewhat lifting the dark, stultifying cloud of religious ideology.

Today's world is still subjected to the belief system founded by the Jewish prophets and Jesus, constituted by Paul and the myriad of biblical scholars after him, and finally formulated by the Roman Catholic Church. Islam as a religion for the Arabs would develop more or less simultaneously, setting the stage for today's religious landscape—and for countless wars and deaths in the name of these religions. All this, based on multiple interpretations of a single god that had its origins as a pagan (nature) god in a small nomadic tribe.

But none of this god's so-called holy books bear his signature. All are intolerant, outdated, inflexible, hopelessly contradictory, and at best filled with obscure passages that can be manipulated to almost any end.

Christianity Today

So: Where is Christianity now? It represents a religion with about 2 billion followers. As of this writing, there are more than 18 significant divisions in Christianity, with a myriad of other churches and sects. Some of these call themselves Christian, and indeed follow Christian ideals, but are not accepted by the rest of Christendom as true believers. The thriving Mormon Church is perhaps the most obvious example.

The central tenets of Christianity in general are a requirement to believe in Jesus as the Son of God, and to find mercy with God. Everything else is more or less optional. It's fair to say that each Christian has their own version of Christianity in his or her head that evolves during his or her lifetime.

The Roman Catholic Church is still governed by a head of state (for the Vatican is recognized as a political state) called the Pope, who is seen as the successor of Peter, the Disciple of Jesus. This man is believed to represent the link between mankind and God, and as such his words are infallible because they are divinely inspired. The Pope typically holds his office for life (though Benedict XVI recently resigned due to ill health, the first Pope to do so in 600 years). When a new pope is required, the cardinals of the Church select him in a succession of votes with the aid of God. But today's Pope has very much become the prisoner of outdated beliefs and practices that cannot adapt to the realities of a modern life. For example, the concept of evolution, accepted as valid throughout science, is still denied, countered by an archaic belief that the Earth is only a few thousand years old. Divorce is a sin, and the use of contraceptives outright banned.

In the 16th century, a new movement arose in opposition to the Catholic Church: Protestantism. They rejected the Pope as a sacred leader of all Christians, and believed that the Bible alone was the true source of their faith. In so doing, they rejected the notion that the Catholic Church was the sole true Church of Christ. The main difference in Protestant doctrine is that said doctrine is "by Scripture alone" and not by papal decree. Justification is by faith alone, and cannot be attained by good works. Salvation comes by grace alone, and forgiveness for sins comes only through Christ.

Today, Protestants represent 800 million of the approximate 2 billion people who identify themselves as Christians. It is believed that there are more than 30,000 distinct Protestant denominations, all with various differences (often quite minor) between their belief structures.

During its early years, the Protestant movement was involved in many bloody clashes with the Catholics, with many killed or persecuted; indeed, in some parts of the world these clashes continue.

The Arabic World before Islam

We've already seen how Moses transformed one of the ancient Hebrew tribal gods into the Jewish God, by elevating Him as the only true god and by merging some of the Egyptian beliefs and rituals with the worship of this God. The same God was to undergo another transformation as a god of the nomads inhabiting the Arabian Peninsula, with an ancient pagan holy shrine of Mecca, forming the spindle of this religion, a god who enjoys more than one billion followers throughout the world today. Where did this god and *his* belief system come from? It's a fascinating story, starting at a small oasis in the desert and radiating outward from there, triggered by an event in which the struggle for survival and access to scant resources touched off one of history's greatest religious transformations—an event that still has a major impact on human society.

To understand this god, we need to go back thousands of years, to the end of the last Ice Age. By then, the glaciers covering most of the Earth's northern latitudes had receded, and the then-lush and water-rich Arabian Peninsula was briefly covered by a shallow sea, before rising again as a barren and desolate land. Before the domestication of the camel, most of the area was uninhabited. It was only after the taming of the camel, with its ability to go for long periods without drinking water and its resistance to heat and ability to carry heavy loads, that humans started to access the region. By 570 BCE, the Arabian Peninsula was sparsely populated, with basic settlements around oases and trade routes linking the northern countries with the then-prosperous Yemen towns, which enjoyed a much more fertile, hospitable climate.

One especially important location lay at the crossing points of the north-south trade route with the trade route from the Red Sea to modern Iraq. A strong-flowing well fed by an aquifer from the surrounding mountains supplied water to travelers. Soon this well also became the nucleus of a settlement, and a water source for the local nomads. Control of this well meant power and prosperity; and various groups, including several Jewish tribes, settled around the well. The Jewish groups most probably settled at the oasis after they were driven out of their previous settlements, sometime after the destruction of the Second Temple in Jerusalem. Being on a trade route, this settlement experienced a continuous influx of people from all over the region.

In 570 CE, the political landscape surrounding the Arabian Peninsula included the Persian Empire in the North and Byzantium in the South. By 500 CE, the tribe of Quraysh had seized control of the oasis, and had come to an agreement to share the water with the Bedouins in the vicinity. Some of the states bordering the Arabian Peninsula were Christian, including Yemen at one point. Judaism was also well established in the Arabian Peninsula, represented by several settlements. Najran in Saudi Arabia was a Jewish stronghold for many centuries before the advent of Christianity.

The Arabic tribes were surrounded by these world powers, then, which were dominated religiously by Christianity and Judaism. Politically, the Arabs were scattered and marginalized, constantly at risk of being attacked and controlled by the powerful nations around them. Their religions still consisted of loosely aggregated myth, super-stition, ritual, animism, and the worship of a variety of gods, some of whom originated among groups in the surrounding countries. Those Arab religions were threatened by the powerful and (relatively) so-phisticated Jewish and Christian belief systems. Their own culture and religion was, therefore, in crisis.

Worse, the Arab tribes were constantly at war with one another other for control of the meager resources available. Life was cheap, and only membership in a specific tribe provided a limited protection. Within these conditions, a new god was to be conceived to replace the existing religions around the well.

The village there, already an important center of religious worship, was to become known as Mecca. In the next few sections, we'll trace the origins of the god Allah and His religion, Islam.

First Religions in Arabia

What gods ruled in Arabia before Islam? Many pre-Islamic sites can still be found in Saudi Arabia, consisting primarily of old circles of rocks, graveyards, cairns, and numerous drawings depicting ritual scenes. Inscriptions are also visible in some rocks, concentrated along the trading routes; these tell us something about the contemporary gods and belief systems originally endemic to the region. Other information includes fragmented writings of Greek writers, Semitic inscriptions, and later depictions in Islamic literature. Even in today's Islam, we can find a few remnants of those ancient beliefs.

The religion in the Arab world then mostly consisted of the worship of idols, with many tribes/regions having their own idol or god. As these tribes were in contact with each other, they also had some knowledge of each other's idols. Some of these idols had many of the characteristics of the Nabatean and other religions prevalent in the countries on the Arab borders. Certain evidence also points to the worship of the sun and moon. Much of the information we have about the idols themselves was recorded by Arab scholar Hisham Al-Kalbi in his book *The Book of Idols* in the year A.D. 821. We know, for instance, that in South Yemen, "Wadd," a love god, was worshipped by the Minaeans. Almaqah was the moon or sun god of the South Arabian Kingdom of Saba. Another significant idol was the Dhu-Al-Khalasah, a carved piece of white quartz that stood close to Mecca. Most of these idols were associated with specific sacrifices, rituals, and rules, some of which linger in modern Islam. These include:

- Animal sacrifice to obtain the blessing of the god.
- Circumambulation (e.g., moving in a circle around a sacred object).
- Shaving of hair and/or donning of special clothing.
- Forbidding menstruating women to come near sacred objects or areas.

As previously mentioned, Mecca, the well where the trade routes crossed, was already an important Arab religious site for thousands of years before the advent of Islam. We no longer know why, for time has erased most traces of the evidence; even the local tribes have long forgotten its religious origins. The one clue we may have is the black stone embedded in the one corner of the Kaaba (a religious building in the center of Mecca), that is circumambulated each year by millions of pilgrims.

This particular black stone has played an important religious role in Mecca ever since the first small shrine was built there. By all accounts, this is the remains of a meteorite that struck Mecca thousands of years ago. The historic oasis dwellers must have been left in awe as the sky seemed to split in a flash of light and smoke, leaving behind this smoldering black stone; it's no surprise that it quickly became an object of worship. Alternatively, the black stone might have been considered special for some reason, i.e., its unique color and feel. As such, it became important and was then transported to Mecca as an idol.

By the time the Prophet Muhammad was born in Mecca, the Kaaba was already in existence, and had hosted many idols. Even if the black stone was never worshipped as an idol itself, it's clear that various tribes brought their own idols to be housed in the Kaaba or close to it. The site surrounding the Kaaba was also holy, with war or killing prohibited on this land, to allow all the different groups to worship their gods in peace. Once a year, many Arab tribes undertook a pilgrimage travel to Mecca to show their respect and also to circumambulate the Kaaba—a ritual repeated even now, as Muslims circumambulate in honor of Allah.

To find some clues regarding the creation of this powerful new god, we need to take a closer look at the most important gods that were worshipped in Mecca then.

The Goddesses of Mecca

Prior to the rise of Muhammed, the most important deities of Mecca were the three goddesses that the Bedouins, including the Quraysh tribe, believed in. The goddesses had their own shrines or temples, similar to the Kaaba, which visitors circled before making animal sacrifices in honor of the goddess. These shrines, all located close to Mecca, included:

1. The shrine of Al-Uzza near Nakhlah
2. The shrine of Allat near Taif
3. The shrine of Manat near Qudayd

The origins of the trio remain unknown, but they were probably imported from nearby civilizations. We can get some understanding of the religious practices in Mecca before the birth of Islam from *The Book of Idols* (Faris, 1952).

> The most ancient of all these idols was Manat. The Arabs used to name [their children] 'Abd-Manat and Zayd-Manat. Manat was erected on the seashore in the vicinity of al-Mushallal in Qudayd, between Medina and Mecca. All the Arabs used to venerate her and sacrifice before her. The Aws and the Khazraj, as well as the inhabitants of Medina and Mecca and their vicinities, used to venerate Manat, sacrifice before her, and bring unto her their offerings. The Aws and the Khazraj, as well as those Arabs among the people of Yathrib and other places who took to their way of life, were wont to go on pilgrimage and observe the vigil at all the appointed places, but not shave their heads. At the end of the pilgrimage, however, when they were about to return home, they would set out to the place where Manat stood, shave their heads, and stay there a while. They did not consider their pilgrimage completed until they visited Manat.

But a revolution was to take place quite soon, and within a few years these goddesses and most other gods were destroyed and forgotten, replaced by the new god Allah. Previously, all the gods co-existed in harmony, with each tribe respecting the gods of the others. That ended with Islam: from that point on, only one god was the true god; all others were false and evil, and would not be tolerated. The new religion and its god would change the religious landscape around Mecca forever; and soon thereafter, Islamic armies would penetrate most of the Arabian Peninsula and the neighboring empires to forcibly introduce the new god and religion.

The Man Who Changed the World

Muhammad was born in 570 CE into the clan of Hisham, in the village of Mecca. His father died when his mother was still pregnant with him, leaving his wife with five camels and a slave girl. His mother passed away when he was six years old, and he was raised by his grandfather, Abd al-Muttalib. We know little about Muhammad's childhood, but we can speculate as to the religious background and influences young Muhammad must have been exposed to.

Being born in Mecca, he experienced and witnessed the religious worshipping around the Kaaba and the constant pilgrimages to this holy place. It is recounted that his grandfather, already very old, had his bedding carried out to the Kaaba, where Muhammad played around him. The rites and practices occurring around the Kaaba must have aroused Muhammad's senses and awareness of religion and gods. Also close to the Kaaba was a strong Jewish community, the so-called "People of the Scripture," as they were called by the Arabs. This was a group with their own distinct religion, teachings, and practices, which served as a stark contrast to the Arab idols/gods that revolved around the Kaaba.

Upon the death of his grandfather, Muhammad, at the age of eight, was passed to his uncle Abu Talib. As a teenager, Muhammad began to accompany his uncle in the caravan trades to the neighboring countries. The trips also exposed Muhammad to Jewish, Christian, and Persian belief systems. According to tradition, at a young age Muhammad met a Christian monk who foresaw that he would be a prophet. All of this must have shaped Muhammad's understanding of religion and of life.

Muhammad, then, had knowledge of his own religion, Arabic religions in general, the religion of the Jews and Christians, and also the dissimilar Persian religion. It's possible that Muhammad might even have been part of a splinter group of Arabs that believed in one god similar to that of the Jews. Within this kaleidoscope of religions, against the political background of Mecca, Muhammad must have reasoned and struggled internally to reconcile the different belief systems surrounding him.

Muhammad was a gifted individual, with a unique ability to unite people and find amicable solutions in challenging situations. One recorded example occurred when the Quraysh decided to renovate the Kaaba, leading to a heated discussion over which tribe was to place the sacred black stone back into its position. Muhammad, returning from a caravan trip, had gone to the Kaaba to perform the circumambulations. Being asked for his advice, he devised a plan to put the black stone in a cloak and have each clan take hold of the edge of the cloak and thus to put it into position.

Muhammad Creates a God for the Arabs

At the age of 40, Muhammad began frequenting a cave on the outskirts of Mecca, in a mountain known as Mount Hira. Why did he want to spend time there? Was it to find solitude, to reason about the purpose of life and to understand the different religions he has been exposed to? A cave setting provides the perfect medium to isolate oneself from everyday life and become more aware of the world, as one's senses and perceptions change in the ambience of the cave and silence of the desert. In the isolation of the cave, Muhammad started formulating his new ideas, seeking answers to the political and religious issues of his day. Using his religious knowledge and internal reasoning, he must have struggled to reconcile the different belief systems he knew, as he worked toward founding a new religion for his people.

The mental struggle of Muhammad culminated in a revelation he experienced one day in the cave. As recorded in the Quran, an angel came to Muhammad as he was lying on the cave's floor. Muhammad first rejected the angel, but it took him in its embrace. By the third time this had occurred, Muhammad had reached his limit of exhaustion and proclaimed as the Angel had asked him to say:

IN the name of the merciful and compassionate God.
READ, in the name of thy Lord!
Who created man from congealed blood!
Read, for thy Lord is most generous!

Who taught the pen!
Taught man what he did not know!

For the first time, the "Word of God" was spoken on the Arabian Peninsula. Muhammad became the mouthpiece of God thereafter. This experience was to be repeated many times over the next 20 years, when Muhammad would have a religious experience or spell during which the words of the new god were revealed.

Let's take a closer look at Muhammad's experience in the cave. Muhammad underwent a moment of enlightenment, prompted by a mental struggle, which culminated in a religious experience and revelation. Was this divine intervention or a psychological reaction to the mental struggle, culminating in a solution? Revelations occur in most religions, and many religious leaders or founders describe an encounter with the divine. But what are these so-called religious experiences? Well, humans may at times undergo peak emotional experiences in which they experience intense feelings of happiness, well-being, inspiration, and awe. In such a moment of clarity, our senses operate at a higher level, and we see our world as from far away. We perceive our world from an altered state of consciousness; and in many instances also experience an awareness of a higher truth, with an intense associated feeling of something unknown or unseen.

Depending on the individual's religious background, he or she may interpret this as a divine or supernatural experience. These experiences normally come on suddenly, and are often triggered by intense feelings of love, the beauty of nature, or meditation. Many of us have had such experiences; perhaps while alone on a mountain, watching the buildup of a thunderstorm, sitting next to a silent stream, finding oneself on a deserted beach early in the morning. The individual is left with a feeling of purpose and elevation. When an individual has been faced with difficult options or decisions, the "answer" may come to him/her in blinding clarity. The individual internalizes the belief as the right one and casts all others away, leaving them relieved, imbued with a sense of purpose.

What was the trigger for Muhammad's revelation? He was wrestling to find answers to the different truths and religions he had come to know. He was also struggling to find a solution to the socio-political struggle of the Arab people. Sitting alone in the cave in the silence of the mountain, seeing the dawn of the day and the emptiness of the desert, must have had a remarkable impact on Muhammad. It awakened his senses and, like a great inventor finally making a breakthrough, Muhammad had a religious experience in the form of an Angel that crushed him and forced him to say God's words: a revelation prompted by his psychological state in the isolation of the cave.

Figure 3: Entrance to the Mt. Hira Cave where Muhammad received his first revelation.

The answer he found lay in the form of a single god, whom he either borrowed from the Jews or elevated from the pantheon already believed in by some of the Arab tribes. For the next 20 years, Muhammad would further this god and his religion.

Today we know more about the neurology of the brain that triggers such spiritual awakenings or experiences. Shahar Arzya et al., in their paper "Why have revelations occurred on mountains? Linking mystical experiences and cognitive neuroscience" (2005) ascribe components like feeling and hearing a presence, seeing a figure, seeing lights, and feeling fear as a result of exposure to altitude and sensory deprivation. These affect the functional and neural mechanisms of the brain to facilitate revelations. It seems that the isolation of a cave, sensory deprivation, and even high altitude bring about changes to the brain that trigger spiritual awakening or peak experiences.

After his initial revelation, Muhammad fled the cave exhausted, thinking he had become possessed, as he heard a voice saying, "*Thou art the messenger of God, and I am Gabriel.*" Muhammad collapsed in the lap of his wife Khadijah, telling her of his ordeal. She comforted him and called for her blind cousin Waraqah, a Christian who possessed much religious wisdom. Waraqah also agreed that Muhammad had been chosen as God's prophet. This was the beginning of the revelation of the Quran, which lasted some 23 years until the death of Muhammad the Prophet.

Noteworthy also is that the Angel Gabriel appeared to Muhammad. Did Muhammad already know about Gabriel from the Jewish scriptures and the Christian religion? Gabriel appears in the book of Daniel, and was also the messenger who brought the message to Mary that she would conceive Jesus. Muhammad must already have been steeped in the beliefs of the Jewish and Christian religions to have conceived of Gabriel; either that, or those who later wrote up the Quran interpreted the angel appearing to Muhammed as the Angel Gabriel.

The First Messages of Muhammad

Muhammad first preached his message to his family and a close circle of friends. Having a good standing in Mecca, and using his charisma, he attracted more people to listen to him. His message consisted of the new religious framework he had constructed during his solitary trips to the Mt. Hira cave, a framework he now believed in after his revelation. His wife became his first convert, and Muhammad slowly built his support base. But his preaching was more than just a religion; it was also a revolutionary movement against the established order. As such, his message quickly attracted opposition, with many in Mecca vehemently opposed to Muhammad's message because it threatened the existing gods and the Kaaba.

As more people began to follow the teachings of Muhammad, the opposition to him grew, and harsh measures began to be taken against those following the new religion. His life was threatened; and after his uncle Abu Talib passed away, most of his protection disappeared. In these difficult times, Muhammad experienced the most intense spiritual experience of his life. During one of his nightly visits to the Kaaba, he fell asleep next to it. In his sleep he was taken by the Angel Gabriel to Jerusalem, and from there ascended to Heaven. In the course of his journey, he spoke with God's earlier prophets, including Abraham, Moses, and Jesus. Finally, he was taken by Gabriel to Allah, where he was instructed by Allah to have his people pray 50 times a day. Upon his descent, Moses argued with him, telling Muhammad that his people would never be able to do that. After going back several times and asking for a reduction, the number of daily prayers was finally reduced to five.

The Jewish prophets and their religion feature overwhelmingly in Muhammad's message. Indeed, his revelations are almost identical to the Jewish and Christian scriptures, from Adam in paradise to the birth of Jesus. This knowledge could only have been gained through intimate contact with the surrounding Christian and Jewish peoples. He also adopted the Judeo-Christian concepts of a Day of Judgment and the resurrection of the dead—new concepts foreign to the old Arab religions.

Indeed, there is a strong possibility that Muhammad may have been educated as an Arab Jewish priest. The message he was spreading was, in essence, that of the Jewish religion. In any case, the Arabs and Jews were virtually indistinguishable from each other, being Semitic peoples with the same languages and physical appearance.

But Muhammad was not a Jew; and for that they rejected him, as the Jewish god was meant only for the Jewish race, the Chosen People. He could preach the Jewish religion, but none of his people would be accepted as Jews. Disillusioned by their rejection, Muhammad slowly turned from being a friend of the Jews to an increasingly hostile opponent. As time passed, his religion became more Arab-centered as he integrated it with existing Arab religious practices. Eventually, Muhammad began preaching that the Jewish and Christian people had been misled, and that their faiths were therefore corrupted from the true and original faith. From the Quran:

God did take a compact from the children of Israel, and raised up of them twelve wardens; and God said, "Verily, I am with you, if ye be steadfast in prayer, and give alms, and believe in my apostles, and assist them, and lend to God a goodly loan; then will I cover your offences and make you enter gardens beneath which rivers flow: and whoso disbelieves after that, he hath erred from the level way."

And for that they broke their compact, we cursed them, and placed in their hearts hardness, so that they perverted the words from their places, and forgot a portion of what they were reminded of.

But thou wilt not cease to light upon treachery amongst them, save a few of them; but pardon them and shun them; verily, God loves the kind.

And of those who say, "Verily, we are Christians, we have taken a compact"; but they have forgotten a portion of what they were reminded of; wherefore have we excited amongst them enmity and hatred till the resurrection day; but God will tell them of what they have done.

O ye people of the Book! Our Apostle has come to you to explain to you much of what ye had hidden of the Book, and to pardon much. There has come to you from God a light, and a perspicuous Book; God guides *thereby those who follow His pleasure to the way of peace, and brings them into a right way.*

They misbelieve who say, 'Verily, God is the Messiah the son of Mary;' say, 'Who has any hold on God, if he wished to destroy the Messiah the son of Mary, and his mother, and those who are on earth altogether?'

In Muhammad's opinion, the Jews and Christians had ignored the signs of God and God's words. Muhammad ventured back in history looking for the real faith before it got corrupted, and thus claimed Abraham to be a Muslim, accepting Abraham as the true one, as below in the Quran:

Say, "As for me, my Lord has guided me to the right way, a right religion,—the faith of Abraham the 'Hanif, for he was not of the idolaters."

Today Muslims consider Muhammad to be the restorer of the uncorrupted original monotheistic faith of Adam, Noah, Abraham, Moses and Jesus.

By 622 CE, Mecca was too dangerous for Muhammad to continue living there, with his life being threatened daily. Located close to Mecca was Yathrib, where he had good support. Yathrib was in political turmoil, however, suffering from constant clashes between two opposing Arab tribes and the then-sizable Jewish community. They needed a strong leader to put an end to their rivalry. Yathrib—today called Medina—offered Muhammad protection, so he ordered his followers (about 70 families) to leave Mecca for Yathrib in small groups as to not attract attention. Muhammad made his escape into the desert just as the Meccans, suspecting a rebellion, attacked his house. This event marks the start of the Islamic calendar.

Muhammad was welcomed in Medina, where he became a politician, administrator, and public adviser. Medinan society was in urgent need of direction and leadership, and Muhammad provided the statesmanship and stability necessary. Yet even with his new status, Muhammad remained humble, living in an ordinary house. Wealth was of no importance to him.

Why was Muhammad so successful in his message in Medina? Because he brought change, and it proved to be the beginning of not only a religious but also a political revolution for the people of Arabia, one that allowed his people to unite and fulfill their political aspirations. As with all revolutions, a certain set of conditions was required to trigger the change, and Medina in 622 provided fertile ground for a revolution. Common features required to spark such a revolution include:

- Popular resentment against the ruling class and their ostentatious lifestyle.
- Such desperate socioeconomic conditions among the common people that they are willing to resort to violence to survive.
- No hope that the existing system can resolve their current conditions.

Most of these conditions prevailed in Medina, and Muhammad was able to bring about much-needed change. By now, the existing Arab religions were confronted by the infusion of new thoughts and ideas from the powerful and influential civilizations around them. The idea of an Almighty God appealed to the Medinans, as this god would protect them from the increasingly hostile city of Mecca, and from other tribes in the region. Most importantly, for the first time they had a religion that was not dependent on the old tribal alliances. In the new religion, both rich and poor were equal before Allah. No longer would the family one was born to determine one's fate; belief in Allah would.

As with most revolutions, the poorest of the poor, the downtrodden and the slaves who had no future, were the first to embrace this religion.

Quite soon, Muhammad had a much larger following. He also succeeded in integrating the Medinan community by reconciling the two warring Arabic tribes, an achievement that later resulted in the Constitution of Medina. This accord defined the relationships between the various groups in this first truly Islamic community. This was a surprisingly modern development, where people came together to resolve a problem rather than resorting to violence. Muhammad proved himself a very capable politician. The one thorn in his side was the Jewish community, which challenged his authority and called him an imposter. They believed that they were the Chosen People of God, and that Muhammad was preaching a blasphemous version of their religion.

By then, Muhammad had come to believe himself to be the messenger of God. It wasn't long before he would move to silence the Jewish opposition.

Jerusalem is Replaced by Mecca

Basically, Muhammad had fused elements of Jewish and Christian beliefs to form his new Arabic religion, and at this stage, he still preached Jerusalem as the center of his religion. But the Kaaba was very dear to the prevailing Arab religions; and in a stroke of genius, Muhammad replaced Jerusalem with the Kaaba. Previously, Muhammad had his followers praying in the direction of Jerusalem; but by divine order, he changed it to the Kaaba. With this he succeeded in integrating existing Arabic beliefs with the Abrahamic religions. The transformation was almost complete for the new religion, the stage set for its explosion across first the Middle East and later the world.

The escape of Muhammad to Medina did not end the hostilities between him and the Quraysh tribe. In fact, the hostilities between Mecca and Medina increased, with both raiding each other's caravans in the fight for diminishing resources in the harsh Arabian landscape. The constant threat of an invasion by Mecca became part of everyday life in Medina—and a successful invasion meant death, torture, and the loss of love ones. This constant threat helped Muhammad consolidate his power and further Islam. Meanwhile, his reforms included military reforms. For the first time, he united Arab tribes to fight as one army, utilizing innovative new military strategies and techniques.

In his book *Islam's First Great General*, Richard Gabriel (2007) describes Muhammad as one of the first leaders to use insurgency to further his gains. The first major battle between the Medinans and Meccans took place at Badr in 624. This conflict became a turning point in the history of the world. Little did those who participated know that this tiny war in an isolated, drought-stricken valley would change the world.

The army of Muhammad was outnumbered by 313 to 1,000 at Badr, but Muhammad was well prepared for the battle. Leveraging his superior military skills, he took up a strong defensive position and eventually achieved victory over the Meccans. His soldiers were battle-hardened and fearless, as they had been assured that, even if they fell on the battlefield, they would attain eternal life in the hereafter. The victory significantly increased Muhammad's standing in the region, and can be seen as the beginning of Islam's expansion. Despite the win, however, the Battle of Badr was not decisive. Indeed, hostilities increased thereafter between Mecca and Medina. In a later battle the Meccans achieved a notable victory, forcing Muhammad and his followers to flee for their lives.

The Jews in Medina, long under threat by Muhammad, seized this opportunity to urge the Meccans to invade Medina. The Meccans raised an army of 10,000 men and unsuccessfully tried to seize the city. When Muhammad discovered that the local Jews had supported the Meccans, his vengeance was swift. The Muslims in Medina began a 25-day siege against the Jewish fortress, after which both sides agreed to arbitration. Muslim General Sa'd ibn Muadh, previously an ally of the Jews, was to judge. Despite objections, he ruled that the Jews be destroyed, as they threatened the safety of the city.

The men were separated from their families and executed, with the women and children enslaved.

Thereafter Judaism was marginalized to make way for the new religion of Muhammad. The first blood spilled to instill this religion was no different than the blood spilled by Moses to establish his own religion, so that *his* God would reign supreme. There was no place for dissent.

Muhammad Enters Mecca

Meanwhile, Mecca was still resisting the leadership of Muhammad, so a different strategy was needed to capture the city. A venerable Arabic tradition provided the way in. All pilgrims to Mecca were offered protection for a few months of the year; and by a custom invariably honored for centuries, no pilgrim could be denied a visit to the Kaaba. So in 628, Muhammad undertook a pilgrimage to the Kaaba, relying on the local tradition to prevent him from being killed or harassed. He set out to the Kaaba with a large retinue, as well as numerous animals for sacrifice. Once near Mecca, he sent out a delegation to negotiate a peaceful visit. The Meccans, knowing the strength of his army, agreed to a 10-year truce.

Muhammad was a master strategist, and although he was not yet strong enough to conquer Mecca, he set about building closer relations with the local Bedouins. His reputation and power grew, as more clan chiefs drew on his support and assistance to resolve quarrels. Slowly he became the unrivalled authority in the region. Even the hostile tribes around Mecca respected him. It was a war for minds and hearts; and unknown to the Meccans, Muhammad was winning the war in the countryside. By contrast, Mecca lacked political unity and central leadership. They were too busy infighting and trying to resolve their internal disputes and rivalries to see the signs of Muhammad's increasing power and influence.

Despite his truce with Mecca, Muhammad supported and aided some of the bandit groups that attacked Meccan caravans. This isolated Mecca further, at least economically. Soon the truce was completely broken, setting the stage for Mecca's final conquest.

Muhammad prepared himself carefully for the final siege, concealing his army and their training from the Meccans. On January 1, 630, he set out from Medina with a force of 3,000 men. As he moved towards Mecca many Bedouin joined him, swelling his forces to 10,000: a mighty army for those days. As his army approached Mecca, the Meccans realized they had been outmaneuvered, and that they had little resistance to offer. In a last, desperate act, they sent a delegation including Muhammad's father-in-law to negotiate a settlement. Muhammad was prepared to declare an amnesty and save those who surrendered. He declared that all those who remained in their houses would be provided protection similar to that offered by the sanctity of the Kaaba.

The message was conveyed to the Meccans, and after a heated argument, the Meccans realized that they had very little chance of beating Muhammed's army, as they were unprepared for battle and surrounded. The Bedouin tribes around them were also cut off, and no support could be expected from them. Soon the streets were deserted, and Muhammad advanced from four directions into Mecca. It wasn't long before the city fell and Muhammad was in full control of the religious center of the Arabian Peninsula. This provided the final opportunity he needed to conclude the initial development of his religion.

Muhammad went to the Kaaba and immediately smashed all the idols (gods) to pieces. Similarly, he ordered all the idols to be destroyed in the local homes: for from then on, he declared, there would be only one god in the lands he controlled, an Arabic version of the Abrahamic God known as Allah. For their own protection, many of the Meccans converted from their various small religions to Islam, as the God of Moses gained power in its new trappings as Allah of the Arab peoples.

To eliminate the possibility of resistance, Muhammad ordered the execution of several people, most of them to settle old scores and to remove the threat of retaliation. Two men who renounced the new god and Islam were also executed, in a very public manner, to serve as examples. Fear reigned in the city; and Muhammad, with his new god, used this fear, the public executions, and suppression to firmly establish Allah—just as Moses had done with his god thousands of years before.

The Conquest of the Old Gods

Now that Muhammad had Medina and Mecca under control, the expansion of Islam could begin in earnest. As with the Jews and Christians who preceded him, there was to be only one God. Those not accepting Him were not only unworthy of Him, they were evil and must be removed as threats to the public good—a concept still alive and well in today's Abrahamic religions.

Most Arabians still revered their stone idols however, so Muhammad systematically began destroying them to make way for Allah. Their destruction is well recorded in *The Book of Idols*. At the time, the three most significant native Arabic gods worshipped were Allat, Al-Uzza, and Manat. Al-Uzza was one of the first to go. When Muhammad captured Mecca, he dispatched Khalid ibn al-Walid to take care of the matter, stating (Faris, 1952):

> *"Go to the valley of Nakhlah; there you will find three trees. Cut down the first one." Khalid went and cut it down. On his return to report, the Prophet asked him saying, "Have you seen anything there?" Khalid replied and said, "No." The Prophet ordered him to return and cut down the second tree. He went and cut it down. On his return to report the Prophet asked him a second time, "Have you seen anything there?" Khalid answered, "No." Thereupon the Prophet ordered him to go back and cut down the third tree. When Khalid arrived on the scene he found an Abyssinian woman with disheveled hair and her hands placed on her shoulder[s], gnashing and grating her teeth. Behind her stood Dubayyah al-Sulami, who was then the custodian of Al-Uzza. When Dubayyah saw Khalid approaching, he said:*
>
> *"O thou Al-Uzza! Remove thy veil and tuck up thy sleeves;*
> *Summon up thy strength and deal Khalid an unmistakable blow.*
> *For unless thou killest him this very day,*
> *Thou shalt be doomed to ignominy and shame."*
>
> *Turning to the woman, Khalid dealt her a blow which severed her head in twain, and lo, she crumbled into ashes. He then cut down the tree and killed Dubayyah the custodian, after which he returned to the Prophet and reported to him his exploit. Thereupon the Prophet said, "That was Al-Uzza. But she is no more. The Arabs shall have none after her. Verily she shall never be worshipped again."*

Manat was destroyed next (Faris, 1952):

> *"When he (Muhammad) was at a distance of four or five nights from Medina, he dispatched 'Ali to destroy her. 'Ali demolished her, took away all her [treasures], and carried them back to the Prophet."*

Allat met the same fate. Muhammad sent one of his people to Taif to destroy her and burn her temple to the ground. The surrounding people were warned not to go back to her under pain of death. Muhammad's Allah was to take her place.

The destruction and removal of other gods on the Arabian Peninsula was merciless and unrelenting. Those rejecting the new God of Muhammad faced death. Believers of the Dhu-al-Khalasah god, in the form of a white quartz idol with a crown, resisted the army of Muhammad. Once his army achieved victory, all the men were slaughtered and the women humiliated (Faris, 1952):

> *"So the Apostle dispatched him to destroy it. He set out until he got to the banu-Ahmas of the Bajilah [tribe] and with them he proceeded to dhu-al-Khalasah. There he was met by the Khath'am and the Bahilah, who resisted him and attempted to defend dhu-al-Khalasah. He, therefore, fought them and killed a hundred men of the Bahilah, its custodians, and many of the Khath'am; while of the banu-Qubafah ibn-'Amir ibn-Khath'am he killed two hundred. Having defeated them and forced them into flight, he demolished the building which stood over dhu-al-Khalasah and set it on fire. A certain woman of the banu-Khath'am thereupon said:*
>
> *"The banu-Umamah, each wielding his spear,*
> *Were slaughtered at al-Wahyab, their abode;*
> *They came to defend their shrine, only to find*
> *Lions with brandished swords clamoring for blood.*
> *The women of the Khath'am were, then, humiliated*
> *By the men of the Ahmas, and abased."*

The armies of Muhammad fanned out over the Arabian Peninsula, destroying any idol god they found. Either by alliance or conquest, the tribes were gradually brought under Muhammad's control. There was little resistance, and for the first time ever, the Arabian Peninsula had a central power uniting it. It was not only a religious revolution, but also a change from the age-old culture of tribes who kept to themselves, with no desire to rule over all the tribes, to a centralized authority.

No other local power opposed Muhammad, and the arid Arabian Peninsula, with its scarce resources, was largely ignored by the world powers.

The Death of Muhammad

Muhammad had bigger ambitions than just Arabia, however, and ten months after the fall of Mecca, he prepared to attack the North. The first expedition failed, as the vast distance and barren landscape proved too much for the army. To expand his support, Muhammad entered into more alliances with local chiefs. Even the local Jewish settlements entered into alliance with him in exchange for his protection.

Muhammad systematically strengthened his position, and soon started having more revelations against those still stubbornly worshipping other gods. They were to be persecuted, and for the first time Muhammad refused them entry to the Kaaba, in contravention of the ancient tradition of providing all believers sanctity. With the threat of Muhammad's army all over Arabia, many tribal chiefs started arriving in Medina to pledge peace with Muhammad and to ask for his protection. In exchange for this, they were forced to accept Allah.

However, Muhammad was never to see the expansion of his ideology beyond Arabia. One day in June 632, he woke up with a violent headache. He spent the night with each of his wives in turn. For the next two days, Muhammad withstood the pain before retiring to his wife Aisha's apartment so she could care for him. In the following days, Muhammad suffered high fever with his headache. Shortly before his death, he performed his last pilgrimage to the Kaaba in Mecca, repeating the ancient rituals that had been performed over hundreds of years, albeit now in the worship of his new god. He lay down, with his head in Aisha's lap, before passing away.

Islam after Muhammad

Muhammad left behind a united but fragile political landscape, fraught with many frail alliances and lingering hostilities. Some of the alliances still favored their old gods, with the lure of Islam weaker in the regions farthest from Mecca. With the death of Muhammad, many tribes felt they no longer had to honor their bonds and alliances with him. The race for succession began immediately after his passing, starting even before he was buried.

Muhammad was the glue that had kept his socio-religious empire together, possessing sufficient statesmanship to unite those whose ideological differences would otherwise have had them at each other's throats. Once he was gone, things began to fall apart. Muhammad appointed no successor; nor did he have any surviving sons. The two main contenders for his position after his death were his father-in-law, Abu Bakr, and his cousin and son-in-law, Ali ibn Abi Talib. A small gathering was called very quickly, without the presence of Ali, where Abu Bakr was chosen as successor.

The Arabic practice back then was that the important men of a tribe would come together after a leader's death to elect a new leader. Realizing the threat from Ali Talib, the group under command of Abu Bakr quickly moved to the house of Fatima (the daughter of Muhammad and wife of Ali) to obtain the allegiance of Ali and his followers. Ali was forced to come out after they set his house on fire. In the ensuing skirmish, however, Fatima was injured, allegedly crushed behind the door along with her unborn son. Only after the death of Fatima did Ali pledge his allegiance, to prevent strife from breaking up the unity Muhammed had so carefully achieved.

Ali himself, however, was firmly convinced of his legitimacy as successor to Muhammad. The struggle for succession after Muhammad's death led to a split in the Muslim community that continues until today, nearly 1,500 years later, with the Shia sect believing Ali to be the true successor, and the Sunni accepting Abu Bakr's succession.

Abu Bakr was faced with immediate challenges. The new Arabian state was still very fragile, with many tribes previously in the alliance returning to their old gods and rituals. Abu Bakr dealt swiftly with this practice, by declaring that those withdrawing from the alliance were denying God, and therefore would be killed. A bigger threat was the emergence of new prophets claiming to be Muhammad's successors. Abu Bakr dealt with this particular threat by declaring that Muhammad was the Khatam al-Anbia, the Seal of the Prophets. The religion could no longer be changed, he announced; the pure Word of God had already been spoken, His religion unerringly revealed to mankind from the beginning.

This belief in Muhammad as the final prophet had a profound impact on Islam. In essence, no more religious development in Islam would be possible or allowed, regardless of changing circumstances and times. For instance, in the time of Muhammad, women were often harassed or exploited. To provide protection, they were therefore not allowed to travel without a guardian (father or brother), a custom which was encoded into the Quran. Today the same rule is still applied in the more traditional Islamic nations, regardless of the fact that security and modern police forces have made such measures unnecessary in most countries. This deliberate stagnation has placed Islam under considerable strain in their efforts to cope with the modern world, in a manner similar to (but often more profound than) that experienced by other religions.

It should be noted that there is some evidence that this notion of Muhammad as the Seal of the Prophets was in fact a later development, rather than an invention of Abu Bakr, and was not originally a revelation as recorded in the Quran.

Abu Bakr lived for two more years, and after his death two other caliphs (successors) continued the expansion of Islam. Ali Talib was finally elected the fourth caliph during turbulent times, after the assassination of his predecessor. He tried to build a broad coalition among the Arabic peoples, but a civil war erupted during his leadership as various groups tried to seize power. In the end, Ali was forced to flee to modern-day Iraq, where he was assassinated with a poisoned sword.

The animosity and division between the two main Islam groups, Sunni and Shia, continued. The Sunnis believed that Abu Bakr and his three successors comprised the true order of succession. The fourth and final caliph was Ali Talib. In contrast, the Shia counted Ali Talib as the first caliph, with his descendants as the second caliph and so forth.

This line of caliphs by inheritance continued until the twelfth Imam, who among the Shia is currently believed to be in hiding. According to their lore, he will return one day to establish the proper Islam, and bring justice and peace to the world.

Today Iran, Azerbaijan, Bahrain, and Iraq are predominantly Shia, with the other Muslim countries predominantly Sunni. Although all use the same Quran, there are vast differences between these two groups.

The biggest schism between the two groups occurred on October 10, 680, during the battle of Karbala. The grandson of Muhammad, Husain ibn Ali, refused the authority of Yazid I, who had been appointed by the third caliph. Yazid insisted that Husain accept him as the true and undisputed caliph, but Husain would not. He lived under an increasing threat of death in Medina, and decided to move with most of his followers, including old people and young children, to Kufa, Iran for more protection.

Two days from Kufu, they were intercepted by Yazid's army and forced to camp at Karbala, where they slowly starved and suffered from horrible thirst. The conditions at the camp became unbearable, with the children complaining constantly of thirst, and slowly becoming dehydrated and dying. Once they were sufficiently weakened, Yazid launched a vicious attack, and the followers of Husain were savagely murdered—including Husain, Husain's six-month-old son, and other children. The survivors were humiliated and taken as prisoners. This event had a profound impact on the Shia; the day is still commemorated yearly by Shia Muslims. Men and woman willingly relive the pain of the atrocities, for the sake of the values Husain sacrificed himself for.

The Spread of Islam and Allah

Between C.E. 634 and 870, Islam was transformed from the first teachings of Muhammad to a major faith of a vast empire stretching from the western Mediterranean region into Central Asia. As new regions were absorbed, their ideas, cultures, and thoughts were assimilated into

Islam. With time, the religion matured and became crystallized in the form we know it today.

Muhammad also left behind new forms of governance, administration, social life, and law, including a tax to be paid by everyone. Most of all, he left behind a trained and massive army. Under the command of Abu Bakr, the army consolidated the new religion within the Arabian Peninsula. War was declared on all who did not obey. Either you honored your obligations with Muhammad and accepted Allah, or you were mercilessly killed; it was that simple. The word of Islam was not spread by apostles, but rather by brilliant and capable Islamic generals. It has been said that the expansion of Islam was more driven by the ambition to expand the Arabic empire than by any intention of spreading the word of Islam.

Whatever the case, the Arabian Peninsula was soon under the Islamic army's control. Each tribe that joined and accepted the new order became part of the Arabic war machine. The Arabian armies swelled in size, and continued to enjoy superb command and strategy. Soon they attacked and destroyed the huge Persian and Byzantine empires, which by then were already in decline. For the first time in history, conquest was not only about land and wealth, but also about ideals. This was a conquest of religion, to replace the existing with a new spiritual framework and god. Islam had arrived in the world.

The Holy Book of Islam

In this final section devoted to Islam, we'll take a look at the Quran, the Islamic sacred text. The Quran is believed to contain the Word of God, as given to Muhammad through the Angel Gabriel. The compilation of the Quran provided the Arabic people with their own book of scriptures equal to that of the Jews and Christians. Indeed, it is based on the same foundation, containing as it does many of the stories and legends of the Jewish religion, with some reference to Jesus as well. The basic references to God, the divine Creation of the world, and the Day of Judgment are identical. As with Moses' teachings, much of the

Quran concerns the foolishness of men as opposed to the everlasting wisdom of God.

According to Islam, life is a daily struggle—a struggle to overcome the temptations in life and to believe in Allah and His way. As with most religions, specific actions and rites are required to maintain Allah's favor, and every step needs to be checked to make sure it does not violate or anger Him. Of course, this sort of struggle is undertaken every day by the majority of the world's population. Regardless of which religion they believe in, most persons question themselves constantly regarding whether they have done the correct deeds as required by their god—a struggle that often increases in intensity as one gets older or death draws near. It's a heavy burden that these gods and religions have brought onto mankind—and the irrationality of some religious concepts have made following them one of the major drivers of human stress and misery.

One difference between the Quran and the Christian Bible is that the Quran is not arranged in chronological order. Rather, it is arranged from the longest verse to the shortest, with each verse connected by a rhyming word. In total it consists of 114 Surahs, as they are known. Although it contains many of the same events as those chronicled in the Bible, its purpose is more to impart the moral lesson behind each particular event than to simply report it.

Muhammad could neither read or write, so you may wonder: what is the origin of the Quran? Its believers hold that as Muhammad received the revelations, they were written down on pieces of bark or tablets, or transmitted orally. When Muhammad received a revelation alone, he would recite it later to his companions. After Muhammad's death in 633 CE, the fragments of his teachings were scattered among the various Arabic tribes, in both written and oral form. It was only after many of his companions were killed in battle that it was realized that his words would soon be forgotten if nothing was done. A concerted effort was then made to collect all the disparate texts and oral transmissions he had left behind. Between 650 and 656, they were compiled by a select group of scholars; and once that was complete, all other forms of his teachings were destroyed to ensure standardization.

It is difficult for the non-Arabic reader to read the Quran, even with knowledge of the Arabic language. Much of its allure lies in its powerful lyrics and rhymes. It contains countless references to the following:

- Religious signs that people are not believing in.
- An emphasis that those who do not believe will be punished.
- That those who ask for signs from Allah are misguided; the signs are already there.
- That salvation will be given if you believe.
- That Allah is great.
- That good things will happen if you follow Him, but very bad things await if you do not.

A great deal of the Quran is dedicated to those going astray from Allah's message. Countless passages in the Quran point to this:

> *Alas for the misbelievers, for their torment is keen! Who love this world's life better than the next, and turn folks from the path of God, and crave to make it crooked; these are in remote error.*
>
> *The reward of those who make war against God and His Apostle, and strive after violence in the earth, is only that they shall be slaughtered or crucified, or their hands cut off and their feet on alternate sides, or that they shall be banished from the land;—that is a disgrace for them in this world, and for them in the next is mighty woe; save for those who repent before ye have them in your power, for know ye that God is forgiving, merciful.*

Many of the teachings of the Quran are evidence of Muhammad's struggle to convince people of his teachings. It recounts countless arguments he must have had with his own people and the Jews regarding the "truth" of his teachings. Most of the verses consist of these arguments and reasoning as to why Allah must be followed.

The Quran also takes a strong stance against any idol gods. After all, the idols comprised the Arab religions Muhammad destroyed to replace with his own.

But when the sacred months are passed away, kill the idolaters wher-
ever ye may find them; and take them, and besiege them, and lie in
wait for them in every place of observation; but if they repent, and are
steadfast in prayer, and give alms, then let them go their way; verily,
God is forgiving and merciful.

And if any one of the idolaters ask thee for aid, then aid him, in
order that he may hear the word of God; then let him reach his place of
safety,—that is, because they are a folk who do not know.

These are two disputants who dispute about their Lord, but those
who misbelieve, for them are cut out garments of fire, there shall be
poured over their heads boiling water, wherewith what is in their bel-
lies shall be dissolved and their skins too, and for them are maces of iron.
Whenever they desire to come forth therefrom through pain, they are
sent back into it: 'And taste ye the torment of the burning!'

Verily, God will make those who believe and do right enter into
gardens beneath which rivers flow; they shall be bedecked therein with
bracelets of gold and with pearls, and their garments therein shall be
of silk, and they shall be guided to the goodly speech, and they shall be
guided to the laudable way.

Verily, those who misbelieve and who turn men away from God's
path and the Sacred Mosque, which we have made for all men alike, the
dweller therein, and the stranger, and he who desires therein profana-
tion with injustice, we will make him taste grievous woe.

In the Quran, Muhammad also laid down a strict moral code for
his people to put an end to often cruel and barbaric practices. These
include:

Thy Lord has decreed that ye shall not serve other than Him; and kind-
ness to one's parents, whether one or both of them reach old age with
thee; and say not to them, 'Fie!' and do not grumble at them, but speak
to them a generous speech. And lower to them the wing of humility
out of compassion, and say, 'O Lord! have compassion on them as they
brought me up when I was little!'

And slay not your children for fear of poverty; we will provide for them; beware! for to slay them is ever a great sin!

And draw not near to the wealth of the orphan, save to improve it, until he reaches the age of puberty, and fulfill your compacts; verily, a compact is ever enquired of. And give full measure when ye measure out, and weigh with a right balance; that is better and a fairer determination.

Criticism of the Quran

As with the Bible, we need to question the authenticity of the Quran. Is the Quran *truly* the word of Allah, pieced together from the revelations that Muhammad received as His mouthpiece? Was every jot and tittle conveyed by an Almighty Who chose to give us His message and His way of life in a single book?

We know that the Quran was compiled long after the death of Muhammad, just as the New Testament emerged long after Christ's crucifixion. Just like the Bible, many of the stories/revelations were retold over and over before being recorded; and we humans are so fallible when it comes to accurately remembering a story. Many times, we flavor the telling with our own interpretations and perceptions, often subconsciously. So how much of the first compilation of the Quran consisted of the inventions and attitudes of the different authors who contributed? Wouldn't it have been much easier if Allah had just given us all a blueprint of a book, signed by Him, that contained all that is expected from us? There would be no more divisions or uncertainty.

Again, much of the lure of the Quran lies in the form in which it has been written, and the way it is read. Even for the uninitiated, the lyrics of the Quran are mesmerizing and captivating. The lyrics are similar to the ancient poems that were used by the tribes to preserve their history and experiences. Like any good song, it touches our emotions and inner self as the lyrics are recited. But it's almost impossible to interpret its accuracy today, unless we unearth indisputable archaeological evidence (and even then, some might dispute it).

I suspect Muhammad himself would be surprised to read the Quran.

Also extremely important to the religion of Islam is the Hadith, or "way of living" of Muhammad. This comes as no surprise. Whenever a country mourns the loss of a great leader, one who has changed them all, there is an almost fanatical collective movement to worship the deeds and sayings of that person. The death of Muhammad had a deep impact on his followers; and as with all heroes, his deeds and actions became larger than life after his death, larger than the person himself. To his followers, Muhammad was more than just a hero; he was also the Prophet of God, the Chosen One. So highly was he revered that his deeds and actions were retold by generation after generation. These became important tools in understanding Islam and its requirements. After all, Muhammad, as Allah's direct representative of God, was the pure example of how life should be lived.

Those people who first recorded the deeds and sayings of Muhammad were his companions, those with him when he was alive. They then passed on those stories to others, who passed them on down the line. Indeed, these sayings, stories, and deeds were passed on almost entirely orally for more than one hundred years; so that by the 9th century, several thousand often-contradictory Hadiths existed in the Islamic world. Finally, Islamic scholars met, then consolidated and selected what they perceive to be the most reliable using various techniques (a similar event occurred in Christianity). Both the Sunni and Shia Hadiths contain differences, however, as each group recognized some narrators as more reliable than others.

It's difficult to judge the authenticity of the Hadiths, since they were recorded long after the death of Muhammad, following generations of oral transmission. A hundred years is an extremely long time in the memory of human beings. There's also significant evidence that in the 9th century, Muslim jurists, increasingly opposed to reliance upon Jewish lore, created new interpretations of the words of the Prophet and his companions that watered down much of their reliance on Jewish sayings and traditions. As the Jewish sources could no longer be used, the next generations of scholars lost their understanding of the context of much of the Quran.

The Hadiths remain a source of controversy in Islam. There are also several contradictions between the Hadiths and the Quran.

What Allah Looks Like

The Islamic God closely resembles the God of Moses, which is unsurprising given that He is, in fact, a transformation of the Jewish god. According to the Quran, Allah has the following characteristics:

- He is a god of reward and punishment. If you do good (believe in him), you are awarded; if you disbelieve, then chastisement waits for you on the day of resurrection.
- He is the god of good, and in a never-ending battle with Satan.
- If you believe, then He will be merciful and take you to Paradise one day.
- He will punish unbelievers, and a terrible fate awaits them.
- All will be resurrected in the day of reckoning.
- Those who do not believe will dwell in Gehenna (Hell).
- He is the only god. No other gods are allowed.
- He cannot be represented by an image or idol. He is omnipresent.
- He is omnipotent, and can make anything happen or change.

Moving On

This ends the discussion of the major modern religions that ultimately trace their origins from the Nile Valley and the Levant during ancient times: the closely-related Abrahamic religions formulated from the ancient beliefs of a small Hebrew tribe, which promoted one of their gods as the only true God. Over time, this god was transformed into the Judeo-Christian Jehovah (a.k.a. Yahweh and The Lord) and the Muslim Allah. Next, we'll take a look at a similar development that occurred in the fertile Indus valley of the Indian subcontinent, the birthplace of the Hindu gods.

The Rise of Hinduism

The gods of the Indus Valley rose long before the God of Moses, with more than one billion followers today. This begs the question of why the God of the Abrahamic religions never appeared to these people, given that it's an article of faith that He is omnipresent.

Whatever the case, like the God of the Jews, Christians, and Muslims, the gods of the Indus Valley also have their origins in ancient ancestral beliefs. Being geographically isolated from the Middle East, the local populations were able to develop their beliefs without the influence of the Abrahamic religions.

The Beginnings of a New Belief System

When the Indian subcontinent crashed into Eurasia millions of years ago, the colliding land masses pushed up the tallest mountain range in the world: the Himalayas. Mountain building continued until as recently as 600,000 years ago. The melting snows in summer, together with the summer monsoon rains, feed a great river that flows inexorably into the arid landscape below. Like the Nile, the Indus River periodically floods its valley, depositing rich sediments ideal for farming, which made it especially attractive to the ancient nomads of the region. As those groups settled in the valley, they gradually underwent the transition from hunter-gatherer to agricultural lifeways. The ever-increasing population also introduced more complicated social structures and thinking, leading to complex belief systems and all the other trappings of civilization.

Archeological excavations have unearthed the remains of human settlements dating as far back as 7,000 BCE on the river banks at Mehrgarh. There is little evidence regarding the beliefs or religion of those people, but in all probability they were similar to Stone Age beliefs elsewhere—including the worshipping of nature and idols, along with animal sacrifices.

By 3,300 BCE the Harrapan culture had developed, with an elementary writing system, urban centers, and an economy. By 1,800 BCE this great civilization was in decline, and archaeological excavations show a deterioration of construction quality and the use of poor build-ing materials. There is still much debate as to the cause of this de-cline—whether it was due to a changing climate, inefficient and inca-pable government, or invasions by other tribes. One controversial and highly-debated theory has a new tribe, the Aryans, arriving from Iran and southern Russia to invade the Indus Valley at around 1,500 BCE, displacing and assimilating the local Dravidians.

It is in this era that archeological evidence shows a change in the local belief structure, as new beliefs became fused with local beliefs to form a new religion focused primarily on sacred fire, with sacrifices made to a variety of gods. Most of this religion consisted of rituals that entranced the attendees with the mystical effects of flame, the darkness of the night, chanting, and the slaughter of animals and sub-sequent blood flow—all rituals that stimulate human emotions and feelings. From these practices, the new gods would arise.

These rituals became highly complex over time, with an ever-grow-ing list of requirements for preparing the sacrificial altar and sacred fire. With the increased complexity, the hymns and chants intended to please the gods also became more elaborate. Soon it all became too complicated for one person to perform, and a professional clergy emerged to administer the rituals and sacrifices. Unsurprisingly, that clergy soon proclaimed itself to be closer to the gods than anyone else, with a higher social standing than most individuals (a position no dif-ferent from that taken by the clergy of other religions).

In the ever-increasing complexity that resulted, as many as 16 priests were required for a public ceremony, with specific roles ranging from the recite to the one who took care of the sacrifice, the chanter of hymns, and more. With time, customary rites developed for every situation, and soon the belief was so widespread that any deviation or oversight might mean reprisal from the gods. Many poems and chants were composed to serve these gods, including some rites and interpre-tations of life—hymns and poems that would become the foundation of a new religion.

The First Writings of the New Gods

At first, these poems or hymns were passed orally from generation to generation, with many authors contributing to their content. During the period from the 15th to the 5th centuries BCE, these verses were written down in Sanskrit, and became known as the Vedas. The Veda texts can be divided into four collections:

1. **The Rig-veda** (Veda of Verses), consisting of about 1028 praise hymns for the various gods;
2. **The Yajur-veda** (Veda of Sacrificial Formulas), containing the different cultic rites;
3. **The Sama-veda** (Veda of Chants), providing musical notation for sacred songs;
4. **The Athar-veda** (Veda of Spells), providing spells and charms to cure diseases and exorcise evil spirits.

These texts became the sacred literature of the developing Hindu religion, similar to the Bible and Quran in being perceived as divinely inspired. Within these texts we find references to the many gods who comprised the Hindu pantheon, and their required sacrifices. Of those named in the Rig-Veda, three are more prominent than the others, in the sense that more hymns were dedicated to them than anyone else. Indra was the god of War, Storms, and Rainfall. Agni was the god of Fire and the Messenger of the Gods; and Soma was associated with a magic drink, its recipe long lost. It was most probably a hallucinatory drug similar to today's opium, which offered entrance to a new world or the granting of godlike powers.

The Rig-veda is a collection of praise songs to the different gods, many of whom have parallels to the Greek gods. This is no real surprise, since both pantheons were created in ancient times in an attempt to label and understand the world around us. These texts also contain the story of the creation of the world. In Hymn 129 of the Rig-veda (Ralph T.H. Griffith, n.d.):

1. THEN was not non-existent nor existent: there was no realm of air,
no sky beyond it. What covered it, and where? and what gave shelter?
Was water there, unfathomed depths of water?

2. Death was not then, nor was there aught immortal: no sign was there, the day's and night's divider. That One Thing, breathless, breathed by its own nature: apart from it was nothing whatsoever.

3. Darkness there was: at first concealed in darkness, this All was indiscriminate chaos. All that existed then was void and formless: by the great power of Warmth was born that Unit.

4. Thereafter rose Desire in the beginning, Desire, the primal seed and germ of Spirit. Sages who searched with their heart's thought discovered the existent's kinship in the non-existent.

5. Who verily knows and who can here declare it, whence it was born and whence comes this creation? The gods are later than this world's production. Who knows then whence it first came into being?

The prominent Veda gods slowly diminished in importance over time, although there are still remnants of them left in today's Hinduism. Indeed, the Veda scripts are still regarded as holy, but are seldom used today. Difficult-to-comprehend notes and commentaries were added in 900-700 BCE by the priesthood to assist them in the rites and their understanding of them. These became known as the Brahmanas, and consist primarily of formulas for rituals and sacrifices, along with their meanings. Each Veda text has one or more corresponding Brahmanah, for a total of 19.

A second transformation of the Hindu scriptures took place in the forests. Away from the distraction and lure of village life, the young priests were taught the Vedic and Brahmanas texts. These were actively discussed between the students and teachers. As such, the literature of the Vedic texts was expanded by more books, namely the Aranyakas (Books of the Forest). These books mostly contain secret rituals along with the meaning and understanding of the rites, with a date of about 700 BCE assigned for their compilation.

The Search for a Higher Truth

In its last phase, the Indus Valley religion was to undergo a change that would alter its structure forever. The Indus religion was characterized by discussions between teacher and student, and as such there were always new ideas mooted and answers sought for questions. It was an evolving religion; and as the Indus society developed and became more sophisticated, the increased power of the existing priesthood was questioned. Also questioned and increasingly frowned upon were the sometimes brutal and bloody sacrifices. The Indus religion gradually underwent an evolution such that a philosophical understanding and interpretation of the world began emerging from the dialogues between student and teacher and teacher with teacher. Whereas the original religion focused on this world—on efforts to increase fertility, ensure good crops, and to protect people from harm—the new thought moved the focus to the world *after* this one. The search for a higher truth had begun.

In this new philosophy, the magnificence of these early thinkers came to the surface. There was a realization that a person's life has four stages or goals, and it is understood that some of us might not complete all four stages. The first goal is that of enjoyment and pleasure, including love and sexual desire. This phase is called *Kama*. We are all born to want pleasure, to be loved, to do things that make us happy, to have many friends, to satisfy our sexual needs. But sooner or later, most of us will seek more out of life. Hinduism does not forbid or deny this stage, but welcomes it as a natural phase in one's life, almost as a necessity to get to the next stage.

After this stage, one's interest turns to seeking worldly success in the form of wealth, fame and power. This is called *Artha*. Many of us go no farther, though there are those of us who are not satisfied and even those of us who pass through this stage and realize we cannot take wealth, fame and power with us into death. Again, this stage is not scorned or despised, but it is seen as a natural development phase.

The third phase is one of renunciation, where wealth and fame is no longer important; nor are the attractions of the physical world. Our needs move from the "I" to the duty of the community, to help the world and those around us, a path of moral duty or *Dharma*.

In the fourth and final stage, we are able to liberate ourselves from all our needs and fears, allowing us freedom from our physical and material world. We have reached *Moksha*.

In addition to the definition of the four stages of life, the new belief structure also argued that one could replace the physical sacrifices to the gods with the reflection of the inner self. Instead of making an external sacrifice to gain the blessings of a god, with a goal of improving one's life or garnering success, one can mentally change one's perception of the world and the inner self, allowing an escape from pain and unhappiness.

A sacrifice is not required to reach this stage. The external world is perceived via sensory aids such as hearing, sight and scent, but ultimately one's inner self, or *Atman*, interprets and perceives the outside world. This soul is the most significant part of the person; the body and external world alike are secondary. The Atman, according to this belief system, is the ultimate entity; one can escape the body and the physical world to free the Atman.

The old rituals and gods are also external in the new Hinduism.

With this revelation, a whole new world of religious philosophy and understanding opened up. Over time, more authors and philosophers added to this emerging philosophy, and many of these ideas and concepts were recorded in the closing books, the Vedanta or Upanishads. Today there are more than 200 Upanishads by different authors and religious schools. The most important and instrumental in shaping the Indus religion are the thirteen main books, however, composed from approximately the 5th century BCE onwards. In contrast to the ritual and sacrifices of the previous books, these books are much more philosophical in approach, discussing the deeper meaning of life, the search for harmony, and the connection between us and the unknown universe or gods.

The New God Brahman

In this new philosophy, the concept of Brahman also emerged. If there are gods, religious scholars reasoned, then who created *them?* Who is above them? The Upanishads advanced the concept of Brahman: an ever-present deity, supreme and absolute, the One we cannot perceive, the One Who is always there. The description of Brahman varies, but is well illustrated in the Maitri Upanishad (Hume, 1921):

17. Verily, in the beginning this world was Brahman, the limitless one—limitless to the east, limitless to the south, limitless to the west, limitless to the north, and above and below, limitless in every direction. Truly, for him east and the other directions exist not, nor across, nor below, nor above.

Incomprehensible is that supreme Soul (Atman), unlimited, unborn, not to be reasoned about, unthinkable—He whose soul is space. In the dissolution of the world He alone remains awake. From that space He, assuredly, awakens this world, which is a mass of thought. It is thought by Him, and in Him it disappears.

His is that shining form which gives heat in yonder sun and which is the brilliant light in a smokeless fire, as also the fire in the stomach which cooks food. For thus has it been said: 'He who is in the fire, and he who is here in the heart, and he who is yonder in the sun—he is one.' To the unity of the One goes he who knows this.

The previous concept of the inner self or Atman was also accommodated with Brahman. Some of the philosophers argued that the Atman is an extension of Brahman.

Reincarnation

Another doctrine that appeared in the new Hindu philosophy was the idea of reincarnation. This concept appeared in the earlier belief system, but it was resurrected, so to speak, in the new philosophy. At the heart of the belief of reincarnation is that the Atman does not die or go to heaven when one's physical form dies, but instead is reborn into another lifeform—and not necessarily as human.

As such, a man who is poor, with a low status in one life, may be reborn as a nobleman in another. There is an endless chain of life, death, and rebirth—unless one can somehow liberate oneself from this cycle. The way to find liberation from rebirth is to find oneness in Brahman, whereupon the Atman becomes a part of Brahman.

The unification of the soul with Brahman is often described by an analogy where a river flows into and merges with the vast expanse of the sea. Some part of the sea has changed due to the river's unification with it, but the sea is still the sea, with its original characteristics. Over the centuries, the way to reach Brahman evolved into a highly organized physical and mental technique called yoga ("to unite"), which was considered a practical means of reaching this stage.

With the acceptance of reincarnation as a central belief in Hinduism, the next logical conclusion was that one's deeds on Earth in a particular life determine the quality of one's next rebirth. This is called the Law of Karma. There is no judge, god, or punishment in this process; rather, the eternal Brahman decides your fate.

The new philosophy reached an apex with the advent of Buddhism, and briefly Hinduism was interrupted. The temporary demise of Hinduism and its gods began sometime between the 6th and early 4th centuries BCE, as the antagonism against the Brahman (priesthood) caste increased, with a revolt against the bloody sacrifices and rituals they deemed necessary. It was a time of intense religious activity and turmoil, and many new sects appeared in northeastern India—sects typically characterized by a charismatic teacher who taught his religious message to a community of followers and supporters. The stage was set for a significant change.

The Preacher Siddhartha Gautama

Siddhartha Gautama, later celebrated as the Buddha, was born in these turbulent times. As with Jesus, it is difficult to separate legend from fact. The story as told was that Buddha was born into a royal family of the Shakya clan. His life was one of comfort and wealth, where no pain or suffering was present. At the age of 16 he married the princess Yashodhara, who would bear him a son. He then had a profound encounter at the age of 29, when he finally got to see life outside the walls of the palace.

As he left the palace on a chariot, he became aware of the poverty and suffering of the people outside. So profound was this impact that he renounced his wealth and family and entered the world outside with only his clothes, which later wore down to rags. After living for six years on the verge of starvation and with the bare minimum necessary for survival, he finally abandoned his life of extremes. He sat in meditation under a tree until he received enlightenment.

Buddha's story is not very different from that of other worldly prophets who had seen the "light," the solution to the world's ills. Buddha was confronted by the world and its cruelty, and he had to find a new mental framework to understand and explain this world. Within the doubts and uncertainties, he finally came to a new insight that clarified the questions and uncertainties. For the next 45 years, Buddha would travel over most of India spreading his message. At the age of 80, he became seriously ill and passed away.

Like all the other central religious figures of his era, Buddha left behind no written works. His message and teachings were transmitted orally from generation to generation, with the first written compilations not appearing until 100-200 years after his death. Ultimately, hundreds of texts were ascribed to him, with several conventions held in centuries thereafter to determine which to accept. We will probably never know the true message of Buddha, just as we will never know the true messages of Jesus Christ or Muhammad. His message was most likely heavily influenced by the religious practices of those transmitting it orally. Later, Buddhism also became highly ritualized.

The teachings of Buddha focused on human suffering and the character of human life. Life is painful, and in many ways our suffering is of our own making, in that desires cause suffering due to our human limitations. By following the path of Buddha, according to the doctrine, one can overcome suffering and attain enlightenment.

Among the most fundamental Buddhist teachings are the four noble truths:

1. Life leads to suffering and pain in one way or another;
2. Our suffering is the result of our desire and craving for worldly pleasures;

3. Our suffering ends only when we liberate ourselves from our desires and cravings;
4. To reach this liberated state, we must follow the path provided by Buddha.

A Code of Ethics

With Buddhism, a code of ethics was also introduced as an aid in reaching liberation.

1. To refrain from taking life;
2. To refrain from taking that which is not given;
3. To refrain from sensual (including sexual) misconduct;
4. To refrain from lying;
5. To refrain from intoxicants that lead to loss of oneself.

We can summarize Buddhism as a philosophy that uses meditation to escape from the realities of the world. Followers hypnotize themselves out of their misery, a technique that psychologists use today. Within it are embedded many of the Upanishad philosophies, and the incorporation of ideas such as Karma and rebirth. Buddhism is an offshoot of the Hindu religion that has almost disappeared from India, but is still very much alive in the areas *around* India. It offers a way for many people to find reason and content in their lives. Today, Buddhism has between 300 and 500 million followers.

Buddhism might have remained a small sect if not for the support of one of the greatest Kings the world has ever seen. In 269 BCE, Ashoka the Great conquered the Indian subcontinent, ruling it until 232 BCE. According to legend, he converted to Buddhism after witnessing the senseless slaughter of thousands of people in the battle of Katinga. Appalled by this sight, and in search of a higher truth where people did not have to kill each other, he became one of the greatest administrators and leaders the world has ever seen. The deeper teachings of the Upanishads and the philosophy of Buddha formed the basis of his beliefs and rule. Under his rule, Buddhism flourished and become the predominant religion of India.

The New Hinduism

By 400 CE, a revival began in classic Hinduism, which had been in decline for centuries. The new Hinduism merged many Buddhist and Jainist concepts; most importantly, its revival would also see an increase in the worship of images, with increasing importance of gods such as Vishnu, Shiva, Krishna, and Rama.

Why did Hinduism return so suddenly? The answer is that Hinduism was never really gone. Although Buddhism became the state religion and spread through the Indian subcontinent, the old rituals and ideas remained popular among the common people, while being influenced by Buddhism. Much of the revival was spearheaded by a gifted philosopher named Adi Shankara. Born in 788 CE, and only living to the age of 32 (according to scholarly dates), his interpretation and insight of the Upanishads, Vedic texts, and Buddhist concepts was to change India forever. In his quest to unite the many ideas and views present in India, he furthered and advanced a new school of Hindu thought, the Advaita Vedanta, that rested firmly on the Upanishads, Brahma Sutra, and an Indian epic, the *Bhagavad Gita*—a new school that would become one of the most (if not *the* most) influential schools of Hindu philosophy. This philosophy taught that the Atman (the soul) and Brahman are one.

With the new creativity and changes in Hinduism, there was also a revival in literature and poetry. In this era, two works appeared that immortalized the religious thoughts and philosophy in epics, namely the *Mahabharata* and *Ramayana*. Whereas the Vedic texts and Upanishads were at times obscure and difficult to interpret, these two epics come to the forefront to teach Hindu principles to the masses. Both are pervasive in India, and it can be safely said that every Hindu has heard of and knows about these epics.

The traditional view of the *Mahabharata* is that it was written 4,000-5,000 years ago, immediately following the events that took place in the epic. Academic thought is that this is a composite work composed by many authors over hundreds of years between 300 BCE and 300 CE. The ethical and religious teachings of Hinduism are interwoven within the epic, as a momentous battle unfolds and its characters are faced with the challenges of life and dialogue with the gods. The ideas of dharma (good deeds), liberation, Moksha, renunciation, and yoga are all embedded within the epic.

One remarkable aspect of these epics is the use of the Socratic way of teaching, as compared to didactic teaching. The Abrahamic religions mostly use didactic teaching: in other words, these are the answers and this is the way, period; go and learn these. The Hindu epics of the *Mahabharata* and *Ramayana*, however, ask numerous questions and debate issues between individuals with opposing viewpoints, in order to illustrate ideas and rational thinking. This allows the individual to understand the issues and more easily place them into the proper context.

With the revival of Hinduism, a new doctrine also emerged that pronounced that people could reject the complex Hindu ritual and religious rites in favor of devotion or love for a god; this was the Bhakti movement. If one truly believes and devotes oneself to a god, then salvation can also be reached, as with the Abrahamic religions. The love or devotion can be to a spiritual leader, or to a specific god, e.g. Shiva, Vishnu, or Shakti. To serve these needs, temples became common in India as places to both house the gods and to worship and show devotion. Yet again, the gods triumphed over logic and reason.

Paths to Salvation

Bhakti became one of the three paths to salvation. The other two, as already discussed, included being one with Brahman (when we realize our identity with Brahman, using meditation or yoga, named as Jnana) and Karma (fulfilling one's social and family duties to outweigh the bad deeds one has performed). The Bhakti path is the path favored by most Indians.

This sort of devotion to a god has its parallels in Judaism, Christianity and Islam. All these religions require devotion to a god to attain salvation. Indeed, in the Abrahamic religions, this is the *only* path allowed to reach God, Allah, or Yahweh. In Christianity, this is currently being challenged; a thesis or belief is developing where deeds or actions are more important than devotion.

The temples and deities in Hinduism also provide us with much insight into the religion. Universally, it is expected that footwear must be removed before entering a temple, with many also requiring the washing of feet or the body before entrance—a ritual also found in Islam. Females should dress conservatively, and males should avoid wearing colorful clothes.

After the worship ritual, the visitor also walks clockwise around the image of the deity (circumambulates). The reader may remark on the similarities of these practices to those of the Kaaba in the Muslim world, where the Muslim pilgrimages also circumambulate the Kaaba. Indeed, there is a school of thought that argues that the ancient Kaaba in Mecca started off as a Hindu temple established by Hindu priests in their travels, before being turned into a mosque by Muhammad the Prophet after the destruction of the deities within.

Making a Deity

Let's return to the Hindu deities. Are they real gods? Well, one can observe the creation of these deities, or at least their representations—quite literally, and amazingly, the creation of gods by mere mortals. The deities are first constructed of clay, wood, or other base materials, then layered with metal and decorations until the final deity is complete. Once created, the deity is transported to a temple. The next stage is to "awaken" the deity by breathing life or the god into it. After many rites, including rehearsing the Veda hymns, bathing the deity, fire sacrifices, and more, the ceremony culminates in the opening of the eyes. Up to this point, the eyes were covered.

The priest or an honored guest chips away the clay sealing the eyes. As the eyes are revealed—sometimes as shining gemstones—the deity is now considered the god itself. A pact is established between the Deity and temple priests; the god agrees to descend into the deity, and the worshippers agree in turn to care for it. From now on the deity will be bathed several times a day, clothed during day and night, and provided with food offerings.

Today's Hinduism has no church or central authority, leading to a myriad of beliefs, rituals, and practices. The absence of a central authority has also ensured its survival, as it was freed from the influence of a single person (e.g. Moses, Paul, or Muhammad) who has made his own conclusions and inventions and declared those to be the ultimate truth. Hinduism accepts many beliefs under one umbrella, in stark contrast to the messengers of the Abrahamic religion claiming to be representatives of God (Moses coming down from the mountain with the message of God, for example, or Muhammad emerging from the Hijra cave).

The other big difference between the Hindu religion and its Abrahamic equivalents is the question of scriptural authority. In Abrahamic religions, the Bible and Quran are seen as the word of God, word by word, and nothing can be rejected, however distasteful. The books are the ultimate authority, and any argument or question must be resolved in compliance with these scriptures. The Hindu scriptures, although important, are not the ultimate authority in Hinduism; where one's sense of justice or fairness is greater, the scripture takes a back seat to a good and justified argument, a trait that has also ensured the religion's continual revival and vitality.

What is Today's Hinduism?

Although Hindu philosophy has soared to dazzling heights, the day-to-day reality is that many Hindus remain bogged down by their religion's many gods and rituals, and have never been able to shift to the deeper philosophy. It is a religion of pseudo-gods, in which the ancient primitive instinct of humanity triumphs over reason. After all, it's so much easier to be devoted to a god than to believe in science and rational thought.

The ordinary Hindu today will worship a particular god to whom he looks for wealth, happiness, rain, and other needs. The particular god differs from family to family and village to village. Current worship can range from the simple to the complex. A typical worship (*puja*) may start with the chanting of mantras (hymns) and the offering of water and the washing of feet to the god or deity. The deity may also be bathed and clothed with the utmost respect. After the deity is made comfortable, it is offered food that may include fruit, incense, and other offerings, combined with the singing of praise songs and hymns. The worship may be ended by an offering in flames (sacred fire).

Among the thousands of deities, there are a few who can be identified as major gods due to the large denominations that serve them. Within the Shaiva tradition, Shiva is the supreme god, also known as the Feared One or Destroyer. Shiva is depicted in many forms, such as a cosmic dancer, a beggar, or a naked ascetic. Paintings show him with matted hair in locks, a blue neck, and a body smeared in white ashes. He is a god with many characteristics, some of them opposing each other as the result of different folklore and beliefs ascribed to him. On the one hand, Shiva is a destroyer of worlds; on the other, he is also the creator of new life and love. Shiva is the end product of many individual teachings and schools.

Another major god is Vishnu, a supreme god who pervades the universe and is the master of past, present, and future. He is also the creator and destroyer of all existences, and rules the universe. Vishnu is depicted as a man with four arms, to show his pervasive and powerful nature. He has cloud-blue skin, with a crown indicating supremacy on his head. A shell is held upright in one left hand, symbolizing his power over the universe. A right hand holds a flat metal disc as a weapon, to show the spiritual mind. His other two hands are holding a ceremonial club showing his divine power and physical strength—and a lotus flower, showing the awakening of the spiritual consciousness within man. Vishnu also incarnates itself in human or animal form with 10 major appearances, as a fish, turtle, boar, dwarf, and so on. Again, the features of this god are very much dependent on the particular denomination or individual.

A List of Gods

This brings us to the end of the discussion on Hinduism. Thus, we can add these gods to our Great List of Gods:

1. Yahweh, the Jewish god with Ibrahim/Moses as founder, with his origins in a nature god worshipped by a small nomadic tribe.
2. God (a.k.a. Jehovah and the Lord), the Christian god with Jesus/Paul as his founder; an offshoot of Judaism.
3. Allah, the Muslim god, with Muhammad as the found of Islam, an offshoot of the Judeo-Christian religions.
4. Shiva, Vishnu, and the thousands of other Hindu gods, the creations of various Hindu authors, with their origins in ancient Indus Valley rituals.

The Perfect Christian, Jewish or Islamic world

One may ask the question to how the perfect Christian, Jewish, or Islamic (i.e., Abrahamic) world might look like. What ideal world do these religions aspire to and work towards? Here are a few characteristics a perfect Abrahamic world might have:

1. All of us would believe in the same God and scripture. No other religion would exist or be allowed;
2. Each person's main goal in life would be to find the grace and mercy of God;
3. There would be no need to explore the world and the universe around us. God created the world, and as such no further understanding is required;
4. Scientific research and development would no longer be required;
5. Any surviving schools would be turned into religious schools, where the main objective would be to teach children the rituals and ways of seeking the acceptance and mercy of God;
6. Rituals or conditions prescribed by the specific scripture (Torah, Bible, or Quran) would become law, to ensure that everyone could go to heaven. These would include daily prayers, following the Ten Commandments of Moses, and compulsory church, mosque, or synagogue attendance; and

7. Modern development would stop, and mankind would slowly degenerate to a primitive state, where food was gathered from nature and all followed the guidelines in the holy books.

Many (failed) attempts have been made to achieve this religious utopia in the past, and they continue today, with communities isolating themselves from the modern world and trying to achieve the above. The Middle Ages was a concerted attempt to do so, slowing the scientific development of the Western world for hundreds of years. Many Muslim Middle Eastern countries have implemented scripture as civil law, in an attempt to recreate the world as described by the holy books. We face a continuous conflict between those who believe the world should be governed as prescribed in their holy books, and the relentless development of humanistic-based culture and technology.

In the next section of this book, we'll look at how these religions perpetuate themselves from one generation to the next, and how they have survived so successfully—thus far. We'll also take a look at the inevitable demise of these archaic belief systems.

CHAPTER 3

The End of Religion

There are finally signs that the veils of the religious dogmas are lifting. The onslaught of science and reason over the ages has gradually dispersed this dark cloud; finally, the nonreligious will be able to speak without fear, to take their rightful place in the world. The time for change is nigh.

God through the Eyes of a Child

Children are born without religion, their brains *tabula rasa*—void of any belief system or knowledge. It is only during infancy and childhood that the brain takes on a particular dogmatic stance, one invariably based on external sources. The child's belief system is formed via the guidance of his caretakers, his experiences with the outside world, and his own internal reasoning process. The child's religion will not be determined by any god in particular, instead being imposed by the society and belief system he is born into.

The first three years of life are critical to the emotional and intellectual development of a child. Within these years, he will learn his language and expected behavior, and develop relationships. During this process, the child's community and/or parents will begin instilling *their* belief systems into the child's reasoning and intellectual processes. A child continuously receives feedback regarding acceptable religious behavior from parents and society, until he learns how to act and conforms to an acceptable religious behavior.

Thus, a child born and raised in Saudi Arabia will most likely be taught Islam and become a Muslim; a child born in Thailand will probably become a Buddhist; a child born in India will embrace Hinduism; and a child of Brasilia will be Christian. All will be taught that their belief is the only true belief. Even very young children from different religions display stark contrasts between one another.

Buddhist novices   *Catholic children*   *Islamic Girl*

Figure 4: Children with different belief systems.

If there is a god, how strange that He (or She) did not hard-code the proper belief into our genetics, to avoid all this confusion and strife! All the young children pictured above have, at a very young age, been transformed into followers of a specific god. How do we do this? To better understand this process, we need to take a look at the various religions.

Children in Christian Families
Early on, the child in a Christian family is taught that there is someone, unseen and very powerful, who watches him all the time. Good children will be rewarded, bad children punished. This is the God Who created everything, the God Who will decide if Mommy or Daddy

and you will be alive tomorrow, the God Who knows *everything*. The child who does something wrong will be told that God is watching him. The child who asks who made the world will be told God did. He will be taught to hold hands and pray for the forgiveness of God. If a family member falls ill, he will participate in prayers. A Children's Bible will be read to him that contains the heroic victories of the good people of God against the evil heathens.

The child will be taught about the birth of Jesus as the Son of God, and will also be taught, in most instances, that all other religions are wrong or bad. Soon the child will attend a Sunday School, where the church will further reinforce his Christian teachings during his formative years. The child will be taught to use his religion to face grief, overcome failures, find purpose, and more. In all probability, the child will play and interact with other Christian children almost exclusively, and may one day marry someone belonging to the same religion.

Children in a Muslim Family

One of the first sounds a child born into a Muslim family hears is the call to prayer. Five times a day, the family is reminded to perform the ancient ritual of praying to Allah. Like the Christian child, the Muslim child is taught that there is someone, unseen and very powerful, who watches him. Good children will be rewarded, and those not believing in Allah will be punished. This is the God Who created everything, the God Who will decide if Mommy or Daddy or you will be alive and looked after tomorrow. Again, any child who does something wrong will be told that Allah is watching him; and the child who asks Who made the world will be told that Allah did so. If a family member falls ill, he will participate in praying for that person.

The child will learn about Muhammad the Prophet of so many years ago, he who brought the Word of Allah to the world, the irrefutable Word that is the absolute, ultimate truth. The child will learn of the contest of Muhammad against the other beliefs of the time, and his ultimate success against them. In most instances, the child will also be taught that all other religions are misguided. Soon the child will learn to read, using the Quran, and once in formal school his Islamic teachings will be reinforced.

The Child in a Hindu Family

As a child born into a Hindu family starts exploring and experiencing the world, he will become aware that most people around him go to a shrine daily. Fruit, flowers, and food are offered to a god, and candles may be lit. The child will be intrigued as he observes family members gathering around the shrine—in many cases, a special place in the house—where they offer praise and prayers. The child will hear the old Vedic verses and will be told the great stories of the gods of the past. Within the storytelling, a moral code and belief system will be conveyed to the child.

The child will be taught how to worship in the shrine, and also to visit the shrine for strength or inspiration when facing a difficult task or situation. He will be taught at first to bring a simple offering, repeating an Upanishad verse or singing a simple song. The world will be explained according to the Hindu scriptures, and he will also witness death, which will be explained to him by the religion. The child will be taught yoga and meditation.

How Religion Uses Our Schools

As part of our cultural heritage, we still teach religion in the vast majority of schools worldwide (even in countries where church and state are supposed to be kept separate). Only a small minority of children escape religious instruction. Most readers of this book will be able to recall their own religious education. Who has not heard at least a prayer during school assembly or before a school sporting event, or even experienced a religious lesson or attended a reading from a religious book? Religious teaching ranges from the extreme (for example, the Islamic Madrasah) to completely secular (non-religious) schools— e.g., the public school system in France.

But even in the most secular of schools, there is a hesitation or a resistance to teach our children anything that directly contradicts scripture, such as human evolution or the formation of the universe. The current religious teaching in schools is a major hindrance to the human race in our attempts to release ourselves from the shackles of archaic beliefs. Let's take a look at schooling in a few countries in order to understand the extent of religious education.

United Kingdom

Nearly half of the United Kingdom's state schools are faith-based. Of the 590 faith-based secondary schools, five are Jewish, two Muslim, and one Sikh; the rest are Church of England (Anglican), Roman Catholic, and other Christian faiths. Most of these schools are required to offer a daily ritual of religious worship. The statistics from the Church of England alone are as follows (England, n.d.)

- Approximately 1 million children attend Church of England schools.
- About 15 million people alive today attended one.
- 4,605 (25%) of all primary and middle schools are Church of England.
- 236 (6.25%) of secondary schools are Church of England.
- With 45 sponsored and 99 converter academies, the Anglican Church is the biggest educational provider in England.
- 564 independent schools declare themselves to be Church of England.

In most cases, these schools offer excellent schooling, with dedicated instructors devoted to teaching and helping these children. Most of these schools are also well structured, and aim to teach basic ethics and morals. However, these children are also instructed in the specific beliefs and teachings of the Church of England. In many cases, the teachers have to prove their alliance to the Church of England by either demonstrating membership or belonging to a congregation before being allowed to serve on the staff.

A child attending these schools is taught to think within the framework of the Church of England's belief system. This is reinforced by morning prayers, as well as symbols or pictures on the walls. Even more, the child, in his attempt not to be an outsider, will be peer pressured into accepting these beliefs.

A child questioning the Christian teachings will be shown the "right" way, as a lost sheep that needs to be returned to the flock. Ultimately, the child can only accept and act as taught by the Christian religion. His role models (the teachers) will also demonstrate their firm belief in the religion they practice, and the child will naturally follow. By the time the child leaves the school he will no longer doubt or question these beliefs. He will one day send his own children to the same religious schools, thereby furthering the cycle of religious behavior.

In the same country, one will find a few Islamic schools. According to the Association of Muslim Schools in the UK (AMSUK) there are now 127 full-time Muslim schools in the UK, including both primary and secondary schools. Many of these schools also offer excellent academic schooling, with dedicated teachers, and the goal of teaching children basic ethics and morals—as practiced in the Islamic belief system. The teachers reinforce and confirm that Islam is the one and only true belief. It is expected that all the children will conform to these beliefs. The child who might question Islam will see himself as wrong, since everyone around him (including the teacher as role model) obviously firmly believes.

Furthermore, he will also be taught that any diversion from Islamic tenets amounts to sin, which will mean no afterlife after his death. By the time the child leaves the school, he will no longer doubt or question these beliefs—and again, he will one day send his own children to the same religious schools.

Iran

An extreme case of religious education can be found in the modern schools of Iran. After the 1979 Islamic revolution, Islam was systematically integrated in the public schools. Courses and textbooks not in line with the mainstream religion were replaced. Secular teachers (those not aligned with Islam) were marginalized or replaced; indeed, more than 700 professors were expelled from Iran's academic institutions. A Supreme Cultural Revolution Council was formed to oversee the integration of Islamic values into education. Belief in Islam became compulsory, and learning the Quran is compulsory in all primary schools. Teachers are screened and must pass a religious examination to be allowed to teach.

Generation after generation is taught the Islamic belief system, with little or no opportunity for children to argue and reason against it.

It is clear from these two examples how education is used to further religion. Education through schools is a vital tool that allows religion to ensure not just its survival, but also its stranglehold on society.

Secular Schools

Ideally, in nations where the church and state are officially separate, schools are operated independently of religion. This ideal is not often met in reality. There are few truly secular schools systems in the world. One exception is France, where the government operates schools that have no communal prayers, religious symbols, or religious assemblies at all. Schools are considered to be neutral places where children are educated away from political or religious pressures and convictions. The quality of the school is based entirely on its administration and quality of its teachers.

Are Religious Kids Happier Than Non-Religious Kids?

Some religious schools claim that their children are happier and better equipped for life, display less drug abuse and antisocial behavior, and have higher moral values and ethics than children educated in secular schools. In August 2001, the University of Notre Dame (a Catholic university) and University of North Carolina conducted a National Study of Youth and Religion in the U.S.A (Christian Smith, 2002). This report begins:

> "This report, based on nationally representative survey data, shows that religious U.S. 12th graders have significantly higher self-esteem

and hold more positive attitudes about life in general than their less religious peers."

The report also claims:

"The 31 percent of all 12th graders who attend religious services weekly and the 30 percent of high school seniors for whom religion is very important are significantly more likely than non-attendees and the nonreligious to:

- have positive attitudes toward themselves
- enjoy life as much as anyone
- feel like their lives are useful
- feel hopeful about their futures
- feel satisfied with their lives
- feel like they have something of which to be proud
- feel good to be alive
- feel like life is meaningful
- enjoy being in school

Assuming this report is accurate and unbiased, does the above findings prove the worthiness and truth of religion, suggesting that without religion we lose track of our moral values. The study also includes the results of a study of Mormon school children. These students were the most engaged in practicing their faith, and a high percentage of them have no or few doubts about religious beliefs, are less likely than other teens to use drugs and alcohol, and are more likely to abstain from premarital sexual relationships.

Other surveys also claim that spiritual people are more likely to report being happy than non-spiritual people, with lower occurrences of depression as well as alcohol and drug use. However, even if their results are accurate, the above surveys are not proof of the existence of a god or of the moral truth of religion, but rather the result of a religion meeting the social needs of an individual. Michael E. Nielsen, in *Religion and Happiness* (Nielsen, n.d.), puts forth the following explanations as to why religious kids may be happier.

1. **Social Support.** Religion provides the individual a group for social support. By identifying yourself with a religion, you gain

entry into and receive solace from this group. In particular, the elderly, sick, or single persons show much more happiness when religious. There is also a belief in the care and love of a god.

2. **Beliefs.** When we believe we have a purpose and goal, our happiness increases. Our worldly pain and suffering is temporary, therefore, as this is only the precursor to a happier life.

3. **God.** We have a personal caregiver. Even if everyone rejects us, our god still loves us and looks after us. We are in contact with our god, who provides solace and love.

Often, religious activity also includes volunteering and charity work. Studies in happiness have identified these as among our most rewarding experiences in terms of making us happy and providing us with a sense of accomplishment, self-worth, and satisfaction.

The perceived increase in happiness among religious/spiritual persons is more the result of the support and love these organizations offer to their members than the result of a god providing that happiness. Organized religion having the Sun as a god will fulfill the same social needs and support as those whose god is Jehovah. The perceived happiness is *not* evidence to the truth of religion, but rather evidence of the value of the support network and organization these religions provide.

A child in a well-functioning religious group will experience the ethos and peer pressure to abstain from drugs, alcohol and other harmful behavior. It is also a close community, where they watch each other to ensure that harmful influences are restricted. Unfortunately, there are negative side effects to some of these groups. The religious dogma is reinforced constantly, criticism is usually not tolerated, and the group may develop inward thinking and also the notion that they are the rightful or chosen ones. Some of these groups or societies may also develop a rigid hierarchical power structure.

The nonreligious child may not have this social protection net, since there are few (if any) organized support groups for the nonreligious. Such a child must depend on his peers and parents to play this support and reinforcement role. One would hope that, as the dogma of religions fades, more support mechanisms will become available for the nonreligious child. Many nonreligious actions are already sponsored by governments: e.g. talks, videos at school, drug education, etc. However, these programs lack the repetitiveness, peer pressure, and intensity of church group activities, and may not be able to compete with them.

It all comes down to the question to whether a person can be happy without religion, since contentment is so important to human well-being.

Which of the following people are the happiest?

- A priest in a monastery performing his religious duty;
- A wealthy businessman with a private jet and big mansion;
- A teacher teaching a class of first-graders;
- A dancer in a ballet troupe;
- The mother of two children;
- A child in a school;
- A hermit living in the desert or forest on his own;
- A member of an undiscovered tribe in the Amazon rainforest; or
- An old man living in a retirement home.

The answer very much depends on the person himself. A large portion of a person's ability to be happy lies in his or her genes. Some people are just born happier than others. Two persons living and working in the same environment will experience different levels of happiness. External circumstances also play a role; for example, having good friends and children you love can make a big difference. Of course, our childhoods also contribute to our predispositions towards happiness. More importantly, perhaps, is how we perceive and experience life. Important factors here may include:

1. Human relationships, with love and support;
2. Feeling appreciated in a community, with a sense of belonging;
3. Sufficient resources to meet basic needs;
4. Life goals and experiences, now and to look forward to;
5. Good health and feeling fit;

6. Having a comfortable house to live in;
7. Having a pet that you love;
8. Having a purpose in life.

We also experience temporary instances of happiness when:

1. Someone praises us;
2. Having lunch with a good friend;
3. Participating in a sport;
4. Walking along the beach;
5. Dancing with someone;
6. Seeing someone you love;
7. Preparing a meal; etc.

In contrast to happiness, we also have feelings and experiences that take away our happiness. These may include:

1. Status anxiety (because your neighbors are more successful and have bigger houses and cars than you);
2. Comparing yourself unfavorably with others;
3. Jealously or hatred;
4. Working for a mean and nasty boss;
5. Not being able to meet your financial needs;
6. Someone you love dying or leaving you.

Sometimes the causes of happiness or unhappiness are beyond our control. A child might be born with a dread disease; someone might get hit by car and end up in a wheelchair; or a woman might lose her husband to cancer. Religion *does* fulfill many of the human needs to be happy, and may console someone when they suffer a loss. However, religion is not the only vehicle or means to be happy in our culture. As we go about constructing a new, nonreligious world, we will also built social structures to meet our social needs for happiness.

The Religious World of the Child

How does a child perceive the world through the filter of the religious beliefs he or she has been taught—beliefs that are taught as the absolute truth? Children constantly question the world around them, delving into its inner workings. They instinctively seek the meaning of life, and the answers to the questions of what are right and wrong.

One day, returning from a trip, my own son of 7 years left a poem on my desk.

"Daddy
oh daddy, oh daddy
you smell fresh as air
oh you snugaly daddy
you bake, so fresh like the best
we go swiming all day long
but this speshel dad
is so nice
but one day you will die
and that will be the sadesd
day of my life
and I will cry forever
Love, "

My own son, with the stroke of a pencil, conveyed so much of his inner world and questions to me.

Children observe and question the world around them, and build their understanding and moral framework in response to their own reasoning and the input they receive from their caregivers.

We can find some answers about the inner life of children in the work of Robert Coles. He explored the spiritual lives of children over a time span of 30 years, via countless interviews and endless fieldwork. His work and recordings give us much insight into the religious view of the world as seen through the eyes of a child. His research included children from various backgrounds, nationalities, and religions, including children from nonreligious parents. His studies illustrate how religion, nationalism, and culture combine to give a child a sense and understanding of life.

How a Child Applies His Religion in Illness or Impending Death
As Cole points out in his book *The Spiritual Life of Children* (1991),
when faced with illness or death:

Children try to understand not only what is happening to them
but why; and in doing that, they call upon the religious life they
have experienced, the spiritual values they have received, as well as
other sources of potential explanation.

Coles' first awareness of religious and spiritual reflection as an aspect of a child's development came early in his residency years, when
he worked as a pediatrician with children who had contracted polio amid an epidemic in Boston during the middle 1950s, just before
the Salk vaccine became available. He provides a striking account of
a child facing possible death or a life as a cripple, describing how this
religious child uses his religion in the face of a crisis. In this extract,
Coles records his discussion with the child (Coles, 1991):

All of a sudden, healthy children had to face the prospect of being
paralyzed and crippled for the rest of their lives. Some of them,
susceptible to the bulbar strain of polio, had their breathing affected and had to be kept alive by a massive iron lung which en-
closes all of the body except the head. The child was being kept
alive by the mechanical action of the iron lung forcing the lungs to
inhale and exhale.

Children observe and very quickly learned their fate. Either
they will improve or become crippled if not dying. It was in this
context where Coles spent many hours listening to these children
and their fears. These children were already facing the questions of
life, wondering why and where their God is, and most importantly
why them.

The one boy, of catholic background and barely clinging to his
life, asked to be recorded as he may be dead by tomorrow. Waking
up with nightmares he would call a nurse in the small hours of
the night to tell her he knew he was dying. On a bright day he remarked that he could be out there with the other healthy children

to play football or other sports. Why me, Why is God doing this to me he kept asking. Can you please talk to me God? Can you help me? I must have done something wrong for you to punish me this way.

His parents were devastated by his illness, crying as they witness the ordeal of their son. The priest will come and say his prayers, calling on God for his mercy and help.

Coles will talk to him about everyday life and future technology, where maybe one day they can have moving pictures and will still be able to hear and see them many years after they have died. During one of the discussions the boy remarked "I pray I won't die. I'd like to live longer." He bargained with God saying "If I stay here, if He lets me, I've told myself—well, I'll thank God every day, every single day, until I do die, every day!"

The boy slowly recovered and one day he was able to leave the iron lung. He was luckier than others who got paralyzed and who became disabled for the rest of their lives. The boy remarked that God must have been testing him and that as such he will be grateful to God forever.

This young boy was already struggling with the questions of life and death. In this inner struggle he used what was available to him: his religious upbringing (having a powerful god at its center), his family support, and his own internal reasoning. He questioned:

1. Why me, of all the kids?
2. What have I done wrong to contract this terrible illness?
3. What can I do to survive this illness?

The doctors could tell him it was a polio virus, how it was transmitted, and the consequences of the illness; but to answer the above questions, he turned to religion, the tool he was taught as a small child. For the first question ,"Why me?", he could only find the answer that God wanted to test him.

The answer to the second question also came naturally. This boy was asking what he had done wrong, and was scrutinizing his past to see where he was at fault. (He had been taught that if he did something wrong, then God would punish him.) Then he began thinking of all the sacrifices he had made for his god, and he got angry and started doubting his faith. His priest and parents comforted him during this ordeal, saying that he must believe in God more strongly. So he tried even harder.

In the next phase he started making promises to God, swearing his allegiance ever more fervently. At one stage he declared, "I'll thank God every day, every single day, until I do die, every day!"

The boy was one of the fortunate few to survive polio and leave the hospital with his mobility intact. During his struggle with this disease, he negotiated with God and used his religion to find answers for his questions about his sickness. At times, he got angry with God; at other times, this same God comforted him.

Other children were not as fortunate in their confrontations with this terrible sickness.

But how does Tony's religion compare against a secular understanding of life, and how can a non-religious child find emotional support during a crisis or when facing death? How does a secular understanding compare against a religious understanding? Consider Table 1.

Question	Religious Answer	Non-religious
Why me, of all the kids?	God is testing me. The plan is to make me a better person or test my faith.	I came into contact with an infected person, so the virus got transmitted to me.
What have I done wrong to get this terrible illness?	I sinned somewhere in the past. I did not believe strongly enough in God.	I have done nothing wrong.
What can I do to get out of this illness?	Strengthen my belief in God, so He can have mercy on me.	Seek medical help; this is my best chance for survival.

Table 1: Secular Understanding of Illness Compared to Religious Understanding

The boy and his parents perceived his survival as a merciful act of God, and no doubt told their friends that God saved their son. It serves as proof of the power of God and their faith. But in the end, it was the iron lung that saved this boy, and the dedicated doctors and hospital staff who worked overtime to assist these children. The human race finally conquered this dreaded sickness because dedicated scientists relentlessly pursued a cure and nearly eradicated the polio virus from the Earth. It was not God who did either. Today, it only takes a few drops of a vaccine placed in a child's mouth to give him or her immunity against this awful disease. Billions of children have been vaccinated in the effort to conquer this virus.

Given what we know, we can postulate how another child, belonging to a different religion, might have endured this illness. A child of Muslim parents would have called on Allah for support. The child brought up in a religion of spirits and ancestor worship might call on the spirits to help him. This child would have the thought process outlined in Table 2.

Question	Religious Answer	Nonreligious
Why me, of all the kids?	A bad spirit got hold of me, or a witch put a spell or curse on me.	I came into contact with an infected person, so the virus got transmitted to me.
What have I done wrong to get this terrible illness?	I angered the spirits and I am being punished. Maybe I did not follow all the rituals or practices to keep the bad spirits away.	I have done nothing wrong.
What can I do to get out of this illness?	Perform a cleansing ceremony and call on the good spirits or ancestors to help me.	Seek medical help. This is my best chance for survival.

Table 2: Comparing Secular Understanding vs. Religious/Spiritual Understanding

Can God Assist Us, and Is He Helping His Followers?

A strong motivation for the belief in a god or the supernatural is the belief that this god can assist us in overcoming sickness, misery, and pain. If everything else fails, then this powerful god can still save or protect us. But do we have evidence of such intervention? Do we have statistics showing that followers of a specific god have a better healing rate than other religious peoples, or that they are more successful in sporting events? If we have four athletes, all with the same physical ability, competing in a race, will the one with the true god have a distinct advantage to the other athletes? If the god is powerful, we can even remove the requirement of having four athletes of the same competency, as god can make even the slowest athlete win.

The athletes are taking up their positions. The athlete raised in a Jewish family prays to Yahweh, the athlete from a Christian background prays to God, the athlete from Islam prays to Allah, and the Hindu athlete to Brahman. The signal sounds for the race to start. Who wins?

There is no creditable statistical evidence to be found anywhere to indicate that those belonging to a specific religion are helped by a god or spirit to win the race. If there were, then we would be able to identify all the winners as Christians, Jews, Islamic, etc. But time after time, an athlete will claim the help of a god in winning a race or game; so clearly, if we have two Christian athletes competing, then the one who is God's favorite will win. But what about the other one; why didn't God favor him? Did he sin more than the other? Was he improperly baptized? Did God just like the other guy better? Of course not. The only support religious belief offers any athlete is psychological; the athlete believes so fervently in God that he orientates his mind to win with the help of God.

What about a plane crash that only a few passengers survive? Do all the survivors belong to a specific religion? Most survivors will claim the mercy of a god to explain their survival. In 2009, a passenger plane crashed in the Indian Ocean close to Mauritius. A total of 151 people perished, but one 13-year-old girl survived. Her father claimed that

God had saved her. But what about the others? Can we tally up the plane crash survivors over the past 20 years and see if one religion gave some survivors a better chance? Again, no. There is no evidence at all to indicate that one religion's god is more powerful than any other's or the only god. If there were such a god, then we would have had hard facts to prove his or her existence by now. The real picture is rather:

Religious	Facts
I survived the plane crash. God looked out for me. He protected me.	Air crash investigation reveals that the survivors were located in the rear end of the plane, away from the impact zone. Seat design and safety measures contributed to their survival.

Over the past few years, many studies have been performed in an attempt to establish a link between religion and health, with different outcomes depending upon the tools and analysis used for the study. However, none of these studies clearly indicate that one religious group has better outcomes than any other religious group.

In a group of one thousand patients with similar heart problems or breast cancer, will those believing in a specific religion have a better recovery rate? The answer is no; there is no relationship between recovery and the belief in a specific god. The recovery rate is a function of the quality of health care received and the initial health of the individual. There is, however, some evidence that positive emotions and/or attitudes can benefit health and well-being. Negative emotions bring about fear, depression, and anxiety, which may adversely affect our body chemistry and functioning to such an extent that it impacts our health: e.g., blood pressure, hormone levels, etc.

The religious person may be emotionally strong, due to his belief that his religion gives him a better chance of recovery. He may also enjoy the benefits of community support. But again, any religion or belief will fulfill this purpose. Statistics show that there is no better strategy for survival during a medical crisis than the use of modern medicine. There are no miracles, no intervention of a god.

Government Sponsored Religion

Religion is entrenched within our governments, as a result of our religious history and the never-ending quest of religious groups to gain and utilize the power of the state. Even in the most developed of nations, religious parties will often contest to be elected. There remains a belief and perception that a religious government will appease its particular god, who will then favor that country.

True separation of church and state has taken hold only in a few countries, and then only after the atrocities of the religious governments reached unimaginable levels of abuse and mismanagement. But even for these countries it is a fragile relationship, with a relentless onslaught against the practice by those subscribing to a specific religion. Overzealous religious governments have generally failed in providing good statesmanship, while strictly secular governments have been much more successful. The rapid development of the Western world in the nineteenth century took place as a result of the strict separation of church and state.

Most governments support or sponsor religion. Even for western democracies, these numbers are high. Of the 27 Western democracies, nine have official religions, with 13 governments supporting one or more religions (Fox, 2008). Some western countries fund clergy, and sometimes even collect taxes on behalf of a religion.

Even in a well-developed country like Norway, the constitution mandates the state religion, and requires more than half of the parliament to confess to the official religion of the state:

Article 2
All inhabitants of the Realm shall have the right to free exercise of their religion.
The Evangelical-Lutheran religion shall remain the official religion of the State. The inhabitants professing it are bound to bring up their children in the same.

Article 4
The King shall at all times profess the Evangelical-Lutheran religion, and uphold and protect the same.

Norwegian society is, however, increasingly becoming non-religious, with the above laws having little practical impact; indeed, data suggests that Norway is now the least religious country in Western Europe.

In Denmark, Christian education is one of the mandatory subjects in the school curriculum, although parents can opt their children out of the class. The Denmark constitution appoints the Evangelical Lutheran Church of Denmark as the official state religion, and the Danish Monarch must be a member of the Church of Denmark. As with Norway, the majority of the population has moved away from religion, with the Euro barometer of the European Commission indicating that only 31% of Danish citizens still believe in a god.

Iceland, Sweden, Italy, etc., follow a similar pattern. Western democracies today are actively supporting and abetting religion; however, the growing realization of rationale and science has severely eroded the support of churches. The United States of America has no official sanctioned religion, a consequence of the influence of European rationalism, the need to unite states with different religious convocations, and Founding Fathers who were secular in their beliefs. Religion is, however, deeply embedded within American society, and court cases abound in which the state sponsors religion or uses government money to support religion. No politician has been able to stand up, claiming to be non-religious, and be elected to office. The Pledge of Allegiance sworn by children in American public schools and at the opening of government functions now reads:

I pledge allegiance to the flag of the United States of America, and to the republic for which it stands, one nation, under God, indivisible, with liberty and justice for all.

The original pledge actually read:

I pledge allegiance to the Flag of the United States of America, and to the Republic for which it stands, one nation indivisible, with liberty and justice for all.

The successful lobbying of religious groups had the words "under God" inserted.

The support of religion by governments increases as one moves east into Asia, with the majority of governments either having an official state religion or supporting religion. The Bangladeshi constitution declares Islam as the official religion, with trust and faith in Allah, although religious freedom is allowed. The Bangladesh government supports religious institutions, and religion is taught in schools. In Malaysia, Muslims must follow Islamic law, with Islamic education compulsory for Muslims. Indonesia requires all public servants to take an oath that they believe in the one and only god. In Burma, Buddhist prayers are mandatory in school.

In the Middle East, there is almost no separation between religion and government, with most governments actively supporting religion. Sharia law is enforced by most governments, and religious laws apply to most or all citizens. Most governments fund the mosques and the clergy, with religious education mandatory. Many of the governments do allow religious minorities and freedom of other religions, albeit with varying levels of restriction. Religion permeates to all spheres of government and life. Speaking out against or criticizing the official religion means death or severe persecution. The full power of the state is used in most of these governments to enforce belief.

The exception to the above is Turkey. For historic reasons, this government actively prohibits and curtails the influence of religion within government. Indeed, it even goes as far as to ban religious political parties.

In general, however, governments worldwide support religion. Religious affiliation of a public person is favored, and support of religious education by governments is widespread. Many governments do recognize that there must be separation between church and state, but the separation is often precarious and always subject to change. Looking back, one can see the consequences of religion using the power of the state to advance its own ideology. The outcomes have been so bloody that they spawned a new movement of enlightenment, and the establishment of secular governments in several countries.

When God Kills

It would be impossible to count the number of people who have been tortured or killed in the name of religion throughout human history. From young girls being sacrificed in primitive rituals, to the Aztecs ripping the hearts out of the conquered to make the sun rise, to the Abrahamic "cleansing" of those with other beliefs—all were victimized by imaginary gods. Some of the most infamous historical accounts of religious genocide come from the European Middle Ages. As Christianity became the official religion of the Roman Empire, a cloud of religious dogma and intolerance descended on Europe. The church became the state and the state the church. The Roman Empire was soon ruled by the church, with the direct oppression of any dissent.

In 1184, the Roman Catholic Church began to be threatened by a series of religious movements appearing in Europe, in opposition to the teachings of the church. Throughout the centuries the church had dealt systematically with heresy (disbelief), often by issuing death edicts against anyone found to be in contravention of its teachings. In this age, however, the new movements became better organized, presenting a threat to the stability and dominance of the Church. To counter the threat, the Pope appointed permanent judges with the power and duty to deal harshly and permanently with any heresy they might identify.

A reign of terror was unleashed in Europe in the name of God.

A papal Inquisitor, appointed by Rome, would arrive in a town to identify any heretics. A grace period was offered for heretics to come forward and plead guilty in return for a lesser sentence. These confessions were used for further investigations, with more people being dragged in front of the Inquisitor. If the accused did not make voluntary admissions, they were induced by solitary confinement, persuasion, and torture. Witnesses in defense of the accused were scarce, as they would also soon be accused of heresy. The victims were tortured systematically, with many ultimately burned at the stake.

Europe was systematically cleansed of any opposition to the church and its teachings. Either you believed or pretended to believe, or you died. The clergy had absolute control, and as a result, any development or advancement in thought and knowledge came to a halt. God failed to rescue those tortured and killed in his name. The poor soul found himself at the mercy of the inquisitors, his anguish and fears unheard as he was tortured, often sadistically, by the followers of God.

One of the largest mass trials and executions took place in Germany in 1626-1631: the Wurzburg Witch Trial. Men, women and even small children from all walks of life were accused of worshipping Satan. A mass hysteria swept across Europe, and more than 900 people were burnt to death or otherwise executed by the order of the church. The prevailing state of affairs is described in a letter from the Chancellor of the Prince-Bishop of Würzburg to a friend in August 1629 (Burr, 1896):

"As to the affair of the witches, which Your Grace thinks brought to an end before this, it has started up afresh, and no words can do justice to it. Ah, the woe and the misery of it—there are still four hundred in the city, high and low, of every rank and sex, nay, even clerics, so strongly accused that they may be arrested at any hour. It is true that, of the people of my Gracious Prince here, some out of all offices and faculties must be executed: clerics, electoral councilors and doctors, city officials, court assessors, several of whom Your Grace knows. There are law students to be arrested. The Prince-Bishop has over forty students who are soon to be pastors; among them thirteen or fourteen are said to be witches. A few days ago a Dean was arrested; two others who were summoned have fled. The notary of our Church consistory, a very learned man, was yesterday arrested and put to the torture. In a word, a third part of the city is surely involved. The richest, most attractive, most prominent, of the clergy are already executed. A week ago a maiden of nineteen was executed, of whom it is everywhere said that she was the fairest in the whole city, and was held by everybody a girl of singular modesty and purity. She will be followed by seven or eight others of the best and most attractive persons... And thus many are put to death for renouncing God and being at the witch-dances, against whom nobody has ever else spoken a word.

To conclude this wretched matter, there are children of three and four years, to the number of three hundred, who are said to have had intercourse with the Devil. I have seen put to death children of seven, promising students of ten, twelve, fourteen, and fifteen. Of the nobles— but I cannot and must not write more of this misery. There are persons of yet higher rank, whom you know, and would marvel to hear of, nay, would scarcely believe it; let justice be done...

P.S. Though there are many wonderful and terrible things happening, it is beyond doubt that, at a place called the Fraw-Rengberg, the Devil in person, with eight thousand of his followers, held an assembly and celebrated mass before them all, administering to his audience (that is, the witches) turnip-rinds and parings in place of the Holy Eucharist. There took place not only foul but most horrible and hideous blasphemies, whereof I shudder to write. It is also true that they all vowed not to be enrolled in the Book of Life, but all agreed to be inscribed by a notary who is well known to me and my colleagues. We hope, too, that the book in which they are enrolled will yet be found, and there is no little search being made for it."

The church created the Devil—and in turn, the Devil took the lives of innocent women, children, and men. All were deaths in the name of religion and Church. The god being worshipped did little to protect the innocent and put a stop to this atrocity. An example of the group of unfortunate victims burned during this travesty is listed below.

- Three play-actors;
- Four innkeepers;
- Three common councilmen of Wurzburg;
- Fourteen vicars of the Cathedral;
- The burgomaster's lady (the wife of the mayor);
- The apothecary's wife and daughter;
- Two choristers of the cathedral;
- Gobel Babelin, "The prettiest girl in town";
- The wife, the two little sons, and the daughter of Councilor Stolzenberg;

- Baunach, the fattest burgher (merchant) in Wurzburg;
- Steinacher, the richest burgher in Wurzburg.

The seventh burning:

- A wandering boy, twelve years of age;
- Four strange men and women, found sleeping in the marketplace.

The thirteenth and fourteenth burnings:

- A little maiden nine years of age;
- A maiden still less than nine;
- Her (the little girl's) sister, their mother, and their aunt;
- A pretty young woman of twenty-four.

The eighteenth burning:

- Two boys of twelve;
- A girl of fifteen.

The nineteenth burning:

- The young heir of the house of Rotenhahn, aged nine;
- A boy of ten;
- A boy, twelve years old.

A letter from the major of Hamburg, Johannes Junius, later himself burned at the stake, to his daughter gives us some insight into these hapless victims (Burr, 1896):

> *"Many hundred thousand good-nights, dearly beloved daughter Veronica. Innocent have I come into prison, innocent have I been tortured, innocent must I die. For whoever comes into the witch prison must become a witch or be tortured until he invents something out of his head—and God pity him—bethinks him of something."*
>
> *And then came also—God in highest heaven have mercy—the executioner, and put the thumbscrews on me, both hands bound together, so that the blood spurted from the nails and everywhere, so that for four weeks I could not use my hands, as you can see from my writing. Thereafter they stripped me, bound my hands behind me, and drew me up on the ladder. Then I thought heaven and earth were at an end. Eight times did they draw me up and let me fall again, so that I suffered terrible agony.*

Then I had to tell what people I had seen. I said that I had not recognized them. "You old rascal, I must set the executioner at you. Say—was not the Chancellor there?" So I said yes. "Who besides?" I had not recognized anybody. So he said: "Take one street after another; begin at the market, go out on one street and back on the next." I had to name several persons there. Then came the long street. I knew nobody. Had to name eight persons there. Then the Zinkenwert—one person more. Then over the upper bridge to the Georgthor, on both sides. Knew nobody again. Did I know nobody in the castle—whoever it might be, I should speak without fear. And thus continuously they asked me on all the streets, though I could not and would not say more. So they gave me to the executioner, told him to strip me, shave me all over, and put me to the torture. "The rascal knows one on the market-place, is with him daily, and yet won't name him." By that they meant Dietmeyer: so I had to name him too.

Good night, for your father Johannes Junius will never see you more. July 24, 1628."

Religious Ideology Replaces Rationality and Science

As religion tightens its grip on the human population, it also restricts our ability to invent and discover the world. As the overriding theme is that of serving and appeasing an invisible god, there is no need for inquiry and critical analysis. Why wonder and inquire, if we know and believe that a god created the world and universe? With this widespread (and widely enforced) attitude, Europe descended into a period of intellectual stagnation with rational enquiry coming to an end. Only in the 1600s did the development in science begin to seriously question some of the existing beliefs. The first primitive telescope was invented, and Galileo Galilei was soon to improve it. This also heralded the start of a new clash between religion and science.

On 7 January 1610, Galileo observed with his telescope "three fixed stars," in a straight line, close to Jupiter. Further observations showed that the "fixed stars" changed their position. Three nights later, on 10 January, Galileo observed one star disappearing, which he explained later as being the result of a star moving behind Jupiter. Within a few days he had the solution. The stars (moons) were orbiting Jupiter. He soon supported the Copernican theory that the Earth itself orbits the Sun, and that the Earth is not the center of the universe. Galileo is considered one of the first to realize that the universe and Earth can be described by physical laws. The prevailing worldview then was described in theological terms, and the causes and results due to the intentions of God.

The development of modern science represented a significant step in the evolution of humankind. In parallel to religion, there was now another framework (physics, chemistry, etc.) for describing the universe. It taught that the physical laws of nature are mathematical, not god-oriented. This new model for describing the world quickly roused the attention, and the ire, of the Catholic Church. It was seen as being in direct opposition to the Church, the Bible, and God. In August 1610, Galileo wrote in a letter to Johannes Kepler:

> *My dear Kepler, I wish that we might laugh at the remarkable stupidity of the common herd. What do you have to say about the principal philosophers of this academy who are filled with the stubbornness of an asp and do not want to look at either the planets, the moon or the telescope, even though I have freely and deliberately offered them the opportunity a thousand times? Truly, just as the asp stops its ears, so do these philosophers shut their eyes to the light of truth."*

Galileo, like so many others, attracted the attention of the Inquisition—and with it, the threat of torture or death. With subsequent trails his books were banned and he was imprisoned. Due to his advanced age, he was placed under house arrest, where he passed away at the age of 77.

Even today, the religious still deny the findings of science when those findings are contrary to their religion's teachings, even when offered evidence and the chance to repeat the observations themselves. Geology provides one of the most straightforward, easy-to-follow examples. While there are still many questions about how and when the

Earth formed, and what has happened to it since, the basic outlines are observable in the rocks and sedimentary layers literally beneath our feet. Many of these layers contain fossils of extinct life, and we've developed sophisticated, consistent techniques to determine their ages. All this offers irrefutable evidence of the Earth's antiquity, which anyone in the clergy can see for himself. However, since the relatively recent creation of the Earth by a god is a central tenet of most religions, the evidence is rejected outright in favor of the theological argument of sudden creation.

A Ray of Light in Religious Europe

The world slowly slipped into an age of stagnation as the God of Moses, now transformed into the God of Christianity and Islam, found wider acceptance. The world was to be seen through the eyes of Moses, with a jealous god controlling the universe and destination. Man's only task was to beg acceptance of this god.

But before then, there was a time when the world was about to burst into the blinding light of reason and understanding. Before the fall of the Roman Empire, men like Socrates, Aristotle, and Plato were developing philosophy into ethics, logic, and science in Ancient Greece. Their cultural inheritors, the Romans, were advanced enough to codify a legal system in which arguments and reason were used to make decisions and judgments. But this burst of enlightenment was not to last. Once the Roman Emperor Constantine accepted Christianity in 313 CE, and later, as the Islamic armies fanned out over the Arabian Peninsula, the Western world became stifled by belief systems that required a god, consistent worship of this god, redemption of man at his hands, and a belief that he had created the entire world in just seven days.

For well over 1,000 years, technological and scientific advancement came to a standstill. The emerging ideas and philosophy of the Greek and Roman cultures were frozen for centuries before a new wave of reason and enlightenment flooded over the Western world, enabling humanity to continue the philosophical, scientific, and humanistic development begun by the Greco-Roman pioneers. Not until the mid-17 century did the smothering religious fog begin to lift, at least for a brief period—a period rightfully known as the Age of Enlightenment. This was not a movement started by one person, but rather a spontaneous development of new ideas and arguments by numerous intellectuals and philosophers to criticize existing values, beliefs, and the church. Reason was advocated as the ultimate authority. For the first time, some individuals were able to break through the dogma of traditional thinking and beliefs to find ideas such as democracy and religious freedom.

This movement was so profound that it changed the Western world forever, and heavily influenced the rest of the world.

The accelerating development of science also advanced this movement. The formulation of the laws of gravitation by Sir Isaac Newton, along with other new discoveries, provided an alternative explanation for the universe that contrasts to the belief that a god controls the universe and everything in it.

Dorinda Outram (2005) describes the Enlightenment as a desire that human affairs be guided by rationale rather than faith, superstition or revelation, that human reason triumph to liberate the individual from custom and unfounded beliefs and worldviews. The Enlightenment foresaw a world viewed through science rather than religion.

During the Enlightenment, a new value system was born that is still viewed by some with skepticism today, as it stands in opposition to religion. But the modern world is based on this new value system; and the United States of America was founded on these principles.

However, the two world wars in the first half of the 20th century, and the subsequent Cold War, put a momentary pause on the further expansion and development of the Enlightenment. Religion regrouped to reclaim its power and authority, particularly using the state and media. But again, the time is ripe for change, where the ideas of the Enlightenment will triumph over age-old beliefs and faiths, in a movement to accelerate our development in science, philosophy, physics, human origins, evolutions, and purpose.

Does Religion Make Us Good?

Most religious people claim or believe that one cannot be a good person without religion—that without religion, the world would descend into chaos. Those outside of religion are evil, they believe, and as such we cannot expect them to be good or kind. There is a fear that evil will prevail if religion disappears. Thus, religion claims ownership of "good"; to be defined as good, one has to belong to a religion. If you lack religion, you cannot be good. Like many religious claims, the argument is circular.

Many of us have worked or otherwise been associated with people who belong to a different religion. Whereas those of other religions are, from a religious viewpoint, perceived to be evil or bad, our personal experience is usually just the opposite. We quickly realize that members of other religions also laugh and joke, and become concerned if they hear about one's sickness or loss. Some people have difficulty in adjusting to the reality that these people, although belonging to a different religion, are also good; this realization sets up a cognitive dissonance (a conflict between belief and reality) that leads them to search for all kinds of ways to reconcile reality with internal beliefs. Possible solutions are that we all have the same god, but have different ways of believing; or that these are good people, and hopefully Jesus will show them the truth before they die. Once one starts interacting with people of other religions, one quickly realizes that we are all humans, with the same feelings of pain, sadness, fear, compassion, love, and more. We all share similar personal, career, and family issues and goals.

But what is "good" in the first place—and *can* we have it without professing a belief in a god? Yes, of course we can. Morality is a human invention, and it varies from group to group. It has its origins in ancient behavior designed to ensure the cohesion and survival of a group. As our early ancestors huddled together for survival, they had to give up some of their egoistic traits to be able to make it as a group. They all had to work together to hunt for food, and stand together to fend off dangerous animals. If a person left the group, his chances for survival and reproduction became extremely slim. The group also punished individuals for selfish behavior. Our sense for morality was developed in response to the survival of the group.

As the concept of morality developed, it also got hardcoded in our genes to some extent; some of us are natural givers, altruistic in behavior. We're also taught expected moral behavior by our peers and caregivers. Children are taught to share, care about others, and to have compassion, which reinforces whatever genetic predispositions they have. Anyone attending a playgroup of two-years-old will observe the never-ending refrain from mothers to share their toys, apologize, be nice, etc. The kids not having these traits will be isolated from the group.

Once we get older, our internal reasoning takes over to reinforce our moral code.

We developed our genetic predispositions to morality in our evolutionary past as a means of survival. Along with this, societies also developed moral frameworks as we started building settlements. Order was required in order for a settlement of a few hundred people to be able to live together. Human life would have been miserable if humans in those settlements were allowed to steal, murder, and rape with impunity; so settled humans had to establish a civil society to ensure harmony in exchange for political authority. Each society developed its own moral code. Later societies developed a code of law, and a police force to enforce these morals or "rules of conduct" to ensure that the society could continue to function.

Morality is manmade, not god-made. God was (and is) used as a fear factor to instill a particular moral code. No religion can claim morality or good as its unique purview. If we were to examine normal bell curves of different populations or beliefs, the result would be the same: some people will naturally be "more good" than others. Some will be less good. The curves would show the percentage of humans applying moral values to their lives to be similar in Judeo-Christian, Hindu, Islamic, or non-religious societies—and some primitive tribes demonstrate the best of moral values. Neither is there a statistically significant difference in moral values between religious believers and atheists.

Our species has developed a complicated moral sense, the basics of which are universal to most cultures and people. Religion took some of these and then added other, sometimes misguided, moral values (e.g., the belief that homosexuality is a sin). Using this, they then built a specific code of moral behavior for their constituents.

There are many types of religious moral frameworks in existence today. For example:

- Tribal moral codes.
- The Law of Moses for Judaism.
- Christianity, adapted from the Law of Moses by Jesus and Paul.
- Islam, adapted from the Law of Moses by Muhammad and others.
- Buddhism, the Code of Life as defined by Siddhartha Gautama.
- Ancient Roman Law of 2,000 years ago.
- Hinduism.

Many of these moral systems fail the universality test, as they may only be applicable to their own constituents and may contain irrational beliefs. There have been recent attempts to define a universal moral code for human beings. The International Humanist and Ethical Union (IHEU) defined humanism as follows:

> *"... a democratic and ethical life stance, which affirms that human beings have the right and responsibility to give meaning and shape to their own lives. It stands for the building of a more humane society through an ethic based on human and other natural values in the spirit of reason and free inquiry through human capabilities. It is not theistic, and it does not accept supernatural views of reality."*

The Council for Secular Humanism defines human values as follows (Humanism, n.d.)

- A conviction that dogmas, ideologies and traditions, whether religious, political or social, must be weighed and tested by each individual and not simply accepted on faith.
- Commitment to the use of critical reason, factual evidence, and scientific methods of inquiry, rather than faith and mysticism,

in seeking solutions to human problems and answers to important human questions.

- A primary concern with fulfillment, growth, and creativity for both the individual and humankind in general.
- A constant search for objective truth, with the understanding that new knowledge and experience constantly alter our imperfect perception of it.
- A concern for this life and a commitment to making it meaningful through better understanding of ourselves, our history, our intellectual and artistic achievements, and the outlooks of those who differ from us.
- A search for viable individual, social, and political principles of ethical conduct, judging them on their ability to enhance human well-being and individual responsibility.
- A conviction that with reason, an open marketplace of ideas, good will, and tolerance, progress can be made in building a better world for ourselves and our children.

We are still living with ancient value systems, some dating back more than 2,000 years ago. Some of the values in these religious value systems are no longer relevant, and some were never acceptable when observed from an objective standpoint. With our newly acquired knowledge of how humans interact, as well as the working of societies and human psychology, we can define a *better* system of values for the human race which meets our emotional and future needs, holding true indefinitely: a value system to provide us direction with which to make moral decisions, based on shared human values and the betterment of mankind. It will not be a passive value system, since history has taught us that those who are too passive very quickly find themselves held hostage to aggression and ideology.

Unfortunately, our species has a small percentage of individuals who exhibit abnormal deviance from social norms. A psychopath may go on a killing and raping spree, or an individual may use violent force to obtain the material goods of a victim. Many times, these actions are the result of mental disorders that are genetically based or triggered by environmental factors. These people show delinquent behavior that falls outside the normal human aspiration to live together with a value system. The society in which these people find themselves must then have mechanisms in place to remove such people and protect their society from them; e.g., a police force and subsequent incarceration and, ideally, rehabilitation of the deviant individuals.

CHAPTER 4

The Story of Life

We need to build a rational new framework for life, one that satisfies our human emotional needs but remains in harmony with science and our observations of the universe, to serve as a bulwark against our ancient religions.

Our Humble Human Beginnings

In the previous chapters, we've seen how the human race invented and developed its religious heritage, as part of its journey from its primitive past and nomadic origins to its first settlements and beyond. These ancient religions still permeate modern life, together with the gods we invented, often very little modified since their origins thousands of years ago. It's about time for further development: for us to rise up, to conquer our ancient religions, to develop a new religious and spiritual revolution.

Change will bring anxiety, both personally and externally. Inevitably, the established religious institutions will push back, in an effort to have their gods and beliefs. But soon, the new and controversial will become the norm. Reason and science will replace myth and religion. Understanding ourselves, and building new support structures that enable us to continue to do so, will replace or transform the religious support structures.

With time, this controversial new philosophy will mature and rise as a powerful alternative to religion. It will give the world a rational voice, aiding those seeking an escape from the shackles of ancient and irrational beliefs. It will provide a framework based on fairness, humanity, and goodness, in harmony with science—as opposed to the hatred and irrationality of existing religions. This framework will propel the human race into a new phase, and will serve us well as we unravel more of the secrets of the universe. It will continue to support us as we start populating the vast universe around us, providing a strong philosophy that can stand firm against the gloom and exclusiveness of religions.

The purpose of this book is to change the religious landscape of the world, and to begin the transition from our ancient religions to this modern framework of understanding, reason, and human values by incorporating modern knowledge of science and human psychology.

We must free ourselves from the rigidity of our religious heritage, and its limited understanding of the world. We must free the world from the suffocating embrace of our all-too-human gods, and to move forward in the development and evolution of human thought and religion.

We need to incorporate the knowledge we have gained in the past few hundred years into this new framework—knowledge that was not available when our religions were founded millennia ago. This will give us a profound advantage over these religions.

The Creation of Our World

The modern model of how the solar system formed represents one of the most profound discoveries made in the past century. The discovery has been so unsettling that none of today's religions have accepted or incorporated it into their belief systems. They prefer to believe that God created the Earth in seven standard days (per the Abrahamic religions), or that Creator Kaang did it (!Kung Bushman), or that a cosmic egg/golden womb broke in two (Hinduism) to form the world. (There are literally hundreds of creation myths). But science tells a wonderful story that is as different from these myths as it could possibly be—and that story is evolving rather than static, for it is based on science rather than guesswork.

In the Western world, the first serious challenge to the theological explanation for the creation of the world came in the early 18th century, when philosopher Immanuel Kant proposed his first theory for the formation of the solar system. Only in the previous few decades had the early scientists and philosophers discovered useful evidence pertaining to this topic. As our tools and instruments became increasingly more sophisticated, we could look farther into space, to witness the formation of other stars similar to our own sun. Our discoveries were pioneered by the invention of the telescope. By the 20th century, we could analyze the chemical composition of space objects falling to the Earth's surface and capture space particles just outside the Earth's atmosphere. With the discovery of radiometric dating, we were able to determine the age of those space particles, as well as meteorites recovered from the Earth's surface, and even rocks recovered from other celestial bodies. We now have a fairly good idea of how our solar system formed.

It was born out of a gigantic cloud of dust and gas, one of many star-forming regions that even now are common throughout the observable universe. About 5.6 billion years ago this cloud, several light years in size, begin to collapse in on itself—possibly due to a random density fluctuation, or the external shock wave of a nearby nova. The process began slowly but soon accelerated, as the increasing gravity of the central mass drew in more and more particles. The rotation of the gas cloud increased as it collapsed, similar to the way a spinning ice skater increases her speed by pulling in her arms. The gas cloud flattened out, as particles found it easier to move along the equator of the developing central body.

Gravity increased in the central body as its mass grew, causing it to grow denser and hotter; eventually, the constituent particles (almost entirely hydrogen gas) were squeezed together so tightly that a thermonuclear chain reaction was ignited at the mass's core. Hydrogen began to fuse into helium, and our Sun was born. Even today, the Sun contains more than 99% of the mass of our entire solar system. Meanwhile, as the Sun was forming, dust particles and gases along the proto-star's equatorial plane grouped together through gravitation attraction to form larger bodies, which eventually collided and stuck together to form still larger bodies; and thus our planets were born—in a process which is repeated daily in the vast universe.

An observer outside the solar system at that time would have seen a big sun with orbiting proto-planets swirling through a cloud of un-counted trillions of rock fragments, icy bodies, and dust particles. As the nuclear reactions in the Sun intensified and spread throughout the new star, it began ejecting a solar wind of particles at high speed. This, in effect, became a huge broom sweeping out most of the remaining unconglomerated particles. Our solar system was born, including our home planet, Earth.

If we were to be able to move away from the Earth faster than the speed of light, we would eventually reach a point in space so far away that only the light radiating from the origins of our solar system would reach us. Given enough time, we could watch the Sun being formed, along with the formation of the Earth as one of the planets. This, then, is the true story of the creation of our solar system, insofar as we un-derstand it at this point. Again, this is a process that is repeated daily in the universe, one that we can witness with our most powerful tele-scopes. The Bible, the Quran, and the Vedic verses contain none of this knowledge, despite claims of supernatural help in the writing of these scriptures. Surely, an omniscient god would know the truth about how the universe formed.

Instead, these Holy Scriptures contain only fables about the cre-ation of the world.

How We Know God Did Not Create Earth

By the end of the 19th century, most scientists (and the rest of the world) still believed the Earth to be only a few thousand years old, an assumption based on chronologies provided in the Bible and calculations made by clergy. But soon, advances in science began challenging even these beliefs. In 1910, Arthur Holmes performed the first uranium-lead dating of rocks, which were to change our views of the Earth forever. The first rock he measured produced an age of 370 million years.

The Holmes technique was elegant and simple in its approach. When a rock is formed, uranium is captured within the rock. Uranium slowly decays to lead over billions of years. Using the ratio of the lead to uranium in the rock, the age of the rock can be roughly determined.

Suddenly, the search was on to find the oldest rocks on the Earth.

Given our planet's history of weathering and tectonic activity, very little (if any) of Earth's original surface remains accessible; but a few very old sites have been discovered. Currently, the oldest rocks known lie in an outcrop on an island in the Acasta River, Canada. Dating has put these rocks at about 3.962 billion years old. Small crystals of zircon have been found in Western Australia that have been dated to an age of 4.404 billion years (+- 8 million years). Using meteorite material and other cross references, the age of the Earth has been determined to be about 4.54 billion years. The age of material found elsewhere in our solar system is determined to be 4.567 billion years old. By working our way through the layers of the Earth, dating each and analyzing them chemically, we can build a very good picture of the history of the Earth. Like pages of some grand book, these layers tell us the history of the Earth, from its origins on.

The first million years in the creation of the Earth was a violent period, and is appropriately called the Hadean era, after the Greek word for Hell (Hades). During the collapse of the gigantic gas cloud that formed the solar system, most of the matter condensed to form the Sun; but due to some local density variations, other large pieces of material clumped together to form proto-planets. These proto-planets were originally just a few kilometers in size. With time, they grew bigger as they attracted more material, some growing big enough to escape the gravitational attraction of the sun, though they remained in its orbit.

As the proto-planet that would become the Earth grew larger from the aggregation of leftover material, it also became hotter due to the energy transferred as more matter collided with it. With additional heating from radioactive materials, the early Earth became molten, and fluid enough to allow movement of the materials that comprised it. The heavier metals mostly sank to the center of the Earth, with the lighter materials rising to the top. The spinning of the large iron core resulted in the Earth developing a magnetic field (magnetosphere). A crust eventually formed on top of this molten mass, with a surrounding atmosphere consisting of hydrogen and helium. This all took place within 10-20 million years.

Shortly afterward, another catastrophe occurred. One of the other proto-planets collided with the proto-Earth. So huge was this body that it *almost* merged with the Earth. In fact, most of the heavier metals of this foreign body did fuse with the Earth, while the rest of the lighter materials (along with some of the Earth's original crust and mantle) were expelled into orbit to form a new body, the Moon. Radiometric dating of Moon rocks shows the Moon to be 30-55 million years younger than the Earth. The Moon also has a lower density, with a composition similar to that of the Earth's mantle.

Because the solar system was still full of debris, both the Earth and Moon got heavily bombarded during this early age. Whereas most of the evidence has been erased from the Earth's surface due to erosion and tectonic activity, the Moon still bears these scars. Peering up at night, one can see them with the naked eye. The heavily bombardment of the Earth by icy bodies also increased the amount of water on the Earth. The early atmosphere of the Earth changed, as the lighter gases escaped the Earth and volcanoes spewed both gases and material onto the surface. About 3.8 billion years ago, the bombardment eased off, as most of the remaining debris in the solar system was cleared away by the solar wind.

A new era started, labeled as the Archaean—the Greek for beginning. This also marked the beginning of a more stable Earth. The Earth was still hot, and volcanic activity was common. By now, though, the crust was overlain by an atmosphere consisting mostly of carbon dioxide, water vapor, and other gases associated with volcanoes. As the planet cooled, the first water clouds formed, and rain started falling, eventually pooling into oceans. We can try to envisage the Earth then as large masses of barren, volcanic lands surrounded by huge oceans. Volcanoes continued to spew gases into the atmosphere. In the Canadian Northwest territories and the Limpopo province in South Africa, we can still find some of the Earth's original rock features, called cratons, typically in the interior of tectonic plates where they have been able to survive the merging and rifting of continents over the eons.

More than anything else, this was to set the stage for the greatest development in the history in the Universe (at least from the human viewpoint!). The first building blocks of life formed in this era—a development so astounding that all of today's millions of species of life can be traced back to it. By now, the evidence for the evolution of life from these humble origins is overwhelming. Evolution is evident everywhere: in fossils, in our DNA, and in the life we observe around us daily.

A Speck of Life in a Primordial Sea

So: where did we come from? We now know how the Earth formed, starting about 5.6 billion years ago, from an irregularity in the density of a huge gas cloud that condensed into a lump of material that attracted other nearby debris until it reached its current size. Along with seven other major planets and a horde of minor ones, the Earth escaped being pulled in by the gravitational force of the Sun, and began revolving around the sun in what was then a very hostile environment. This newly formed planet was not very different from the millions of other planets scattered throughout the galaxy. But its specific distance from the sun was to set it apart from the others, because it was neither too cold nor too hot. The temperature range was ideal to favor the formation of certain chemical bonds. So unique was this position that the new planet was destined to teem with life once the surface cooled off enough.

Mankind, throughout its existence, has stumbled upon or un-earthed strange-looking and fossilized bones, or the outlines of crea-tures long extinct. Miners going deep into the Earth will at times, un-earth such fossils. Drills going even deeper into the Earth's crust, into a seam of coal or pool of oil, will often bring up samples containing microscopic remains, evidence of creatures belonging to a long-gone era. Some are found so deep, entombed under so many layers of soil and rock, that they suggest hundreds of millions if not *billions* of years of evolutionary development.

Once radiometric dating was invented, it became possible to date the age of both fossil-bearing rocks and the fossils themselves, and we could start constructing in earnest the evolutionary tale of life as it unfolded over nearly four billion years.

Fossilization is a rare event, requiring very specific circumstances. The dead animal or plant must be covered almost immediately by sedi-ment, with very specific conditions to favor fossilization. It also needs to survive flood, volcanic, and seismic events over the ages. Then it needs to be discovered. Most early life left little evidence behind, as it consisted only of soft tissue. It's no surprise, then, that our current fossil record is still incomplete. But regardless, we have unearthed a rich variety of fossils showing how life evolved on our planet. By dat-ing and sorting these fossils, we can witness the development of life on Earth.

Simpler life forms are found in layers below advanced life, and the fossil record reveals a successive evolution of life on Earth over literally billions of years. There are no seven-day miracles; there is no sudden creation by supernatural entities.

The modern biosphere of Earth is the result of the continued evo-lution of life to fit existing environments, and has been generally pro-gressive from the simple to the more complex.

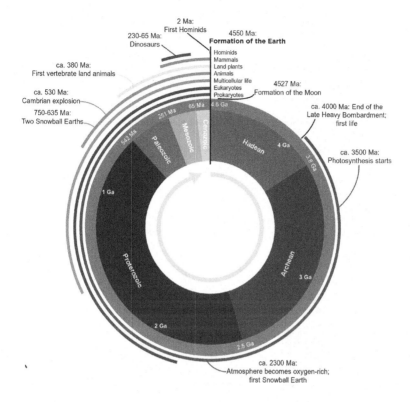

Figure 5: The geologic time scale, showing major evolutionary events.

We do have fairly complete fossil records of some specific types of animals, with the horse serving as one of the best examples. The horse began as a small animal in North America about 54 million years ago. As the climate of the Earth changed, it evolved into the modern horse, via significant alterations in body plan and size. The development of the horse over the past 54 million years is outlined in Figure 6.

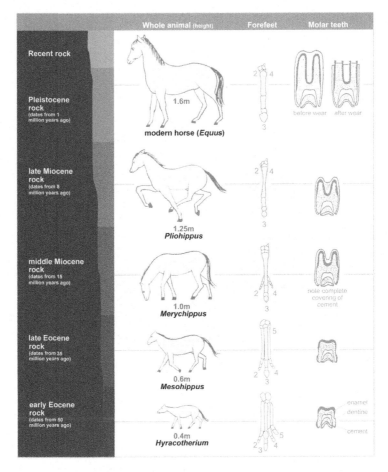

Figure 6: The generalized evolution of the horse

The oldest fossil ever found, that of a single-celled bacterium discovered in Western Australia, dates back 3.45 billion years. These simple microbes consumed the water, carbon dioxide, and sunlight that were present in great abundance on Earth for almost two billion years. The oldest multicellular fossil dates to about 2.1 billion years ago. Animal life, in the form of a primitive sponge, began about 650 million years ago. The fossil record undeniably shows a gradual evolution from the simplest of life to the complex organisms of today. The facts are indisputable. Why would a god stack fossils from the simplest to the more complex in successive layers, according to their ages?

We also now have fossil evidence suggesting how animal life moved from the sea to land. In 2004, a 383-million-year-old, well-preserved fossil was found on Ellesmere Island in North Canada. The fossil had the characteristics of a fish, but the front fins had wrist bones and simple fingers, typical of the kind used to bear weight. Its neck was also able to move independently. This was a fish that lived in shallow waters, one that had to adapt in order to survive. It's postulated that these shallow waters were poor in oxygen, as evident from the layers of sediment around the fossil. To catch prey and to survive, the "fish" used its foremost fins to prop itself up and propel itself forward. The evolutionary migration from water to land was in progress.

This fish (the tiktaalik) had begun to adapt to peek above the water's surface. For this purpose, the eyes and nostrils evolved to lie at the top of the skull. It could move its head around and get oxygen from both water and air. Its bones became sturdier, and soon it evolved further as the animal started scurrying after prey or moved from one pond to another. Features were developing which would eventually result in anatomically modern human beings—in other words, us.

Figure 7: Fish developing adaptations to oxygen-poor shallow-water

There's plenty of other evidence suggesting how we developed. If we take a look at the living organisms around us, we're struck by the many similarities between them. Take flowers, for instance: they all have a basic structure consisting of a stamen, pistil, ovary, sepals and petals. They may have different colors and additional structures, but they all function using the same basic method. Animals all have respiratory systems designed to absorb oxygen, eyes to see, ears to hear, and similar genitalia (testes or ovary, penis or vagina) to reproduce. In a general way, the amount of resemblance between two organisms shows how closely they're related to each other in evolutionary terms. Typically, the less two species they have in common, the further back in time their ancestors diverged from each other.

The bones of bats, horses, birds, and humans are very similar, demonstrating a common ancestry. Below is a chart showing the structural similarities between the forelimbs of salamanders, turtles, alligators, birds, bats, whales, moles, and humans.

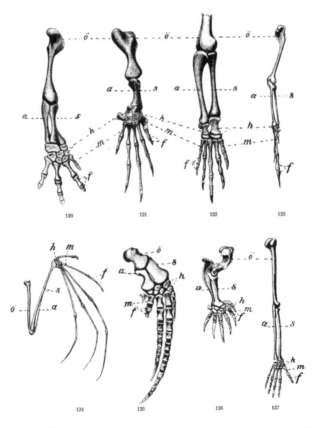

Figure 8: Homologies of the forelimb among vertebrates, providing evidence for evolution

The more similar the anatomical features between two creatures, the more closely the organisms are related and the better the chance that they share a common ancestor. The similar anatomical features derive from the original features of the common ancestor, different populations of which adapted and evolved over time into different species. Admittedly, there are some exceptions to this rule, in which different branches of the evolutionary tree have "converged," or developed independently to possess features that are very much alike. For example, the methods that baleen whales and flamingos have evolved to strain food out of water are quite similar, but the two species are obviously not closely related.

Observing these anatomical features, we also notice that many of the body parts are far from perfect, as Creationists claim they should have been from the beginning. Clearly, these are adapted versions of an inherited structure—versions that often work just well enough to get by, and no better. For example, we humans struggle with our weak backs, as the human spine is not designed for walking upright—and our skeletons have not yet evolved to deal with this. We also possess vestigial parts or features that have not yet been removed by evolution. For example, the human body includes a coccyx (tailbone)—the remnant of a lost tail—and ear muscles that are no longer used. We get goose bumps, which are the remains of an ancient animal trait intended to make hair rise to frighten off predators. Humans have an appendix, a completely functionless organ. In our evolution along the mammal branch, we have not been able to get rid of it. Sometimes it kills us—but other mammals still require an appendix to digest vegetable cellulose with the help of bacteria.

There's an endless list of redundant parts in humans and other animals. In a whale, for example, one can still find the leg bones at the back of the body—the remnants of hind legs, from the days when its distant ancestors still lived on land.

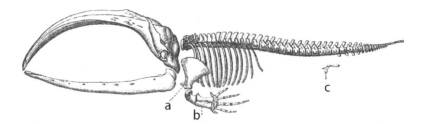

Figure 9: The Letter "c" in the image indicates the undeveloped hind legs of a baleen whale

But there is other evidence of our evolutionary past, in addition to fossils and structural similarities. We see this in embryonic development. Once the male's sperm enters the female's egg, rapid cell division begins as the embryo starts developing. By comparing the development between different organisms along the embryonic path, more evidence of our evolutionary origins is revealed. In vertebrates (organisms with backbones—e.g. most fishes, and all amphibians, reptiles, mammals, and birds), the embryos look very similar in the early stages, before becoming more differentiated at later stages. The similarities are no coincidence; we all share a generalized developmental pattern inherited from a common ancestor.

The differences that manifest later result from modifications the specific species have undergone to adapt to their environments. Human embryos develop a gill slit in the early stages, which later disappears— a relic of the fish ancestor from which all vertebrates evolved. Human embryos also show a well-defined tail that reaches maximum length at six weeks. The tail later shortens and is left as the coccyx.

In general, the appearance of evolutionary structures in an embryo coincide with the evolutionary development of the species. If the evolutionary structure evolved early, it also predates later embryonic development. In humans, the forebrain develops last.

One may ask why the human embryo mimics the evolutionary path in its development. Again, the reason is most probably that the development of the embryo is inherited from our ancestors. It inherited the features of a fish from our fish ancestor; but development continues after the fish features have formed, as other genes are switched on to develop some of those features further or to make them disappear. The embryo uses what has already been developed by evolution, and then sculpts it to fit its needs.

Even more astounding is that just after fertilization, when the first dividing cells become a hollow ball (blastula), a hole or pore develops in the ball. The further development of this pore divides the animal kingdom in two. If the pore becomes a mouth, the organism will belong to the invertebrate group: e.g. insects, worms, and mollusks. If this first pore becomes an anus, the organism is a vertebrate. This development speaks of a long-ago divergence in some common ancestor.

The distribution of plants and animals across the planet also provides support for evolution. Life is not spread uniformly across the land surface; instead, we find that species are often unique to a particular continent or island. In Africa, the plants (flora) and animals (fauna) are different from those in North America (or at least, they were before European contact). Some species may be related, but they are no longer the same. If life was created by the supernatural all at once, and just a few thousand years ago at that, we should find identical crocodilians or just one type of fruit fly on all continents. Clearly, this is not the case; so why are the species so different?

Again, evolution provides the answer. From our study of geology, we know that at different stages in the far past, most or all of the landmasses were united, before slowly breaking apart again to form different continents through the process of plate tectonics. At some point, the same species of crocodilian might have inhabited the entire super-continent; but once that continent broke up and drifted apart, each population was on its own. Each population continued to evolve, to adapt to the climatic changes of the new landmass it found itself on. Multiply this process by millions of different species of both flora and fauna, and you get the incredible biodiversity we experience today. Species separated by oceans may be distantly related, but only distantly; each is a biologically separate species.

The theory is well supported by the life on oceanic islands, and in fact Darwin formulated his theory of evolution based on his experiences in the Galapagos Islands. Many of the oceanic islands formed by volcanic activity are relatively young. When we study the life on these islands, it's easy to see how closely related the plants and animals are. Life arrived on these islands from the landmasses closest to them, either by floating in the sea (as seeds, or animals on rafts of vegetation) or by air. Once they reached the island, they began evolving to make up the unique biological groupings found on these islands.

We therefore have the following evidence of evolution:

1. The presence of fossils in sequential geological layers, from simple life to the more complex.
2. Similar bodily structures in living organisms.
3. The presence of redundant body parts.
4. The sequence of embryonic development.
5. The distribution of species across the Earth.

The diversity of life on Earth today is astonishing. The number of different species across the planet is estimated to be 10-30 million, with more than 1.9 million species catalogued and named so far. There are several online databases where the reader can browse and view these species:

1. Catalogue of Life (http://www.catalogueoflife.org)
2. Encyclopedia of Life (http://www.eol.org/)
3. Tree of Life (http://tolweb.org)

These species range from microscopic bacteria to lichens in Antarctica, from tiny blind cave fish to blue whales, from insects to animals. They come in all sizes and forms. Some of the mobile among them use scent to hunt; some can detect the minute vibrations of an insect wing; some float in or propel themselves through the world's oceans; some drift in the sky; some root themselves in the ground and stay in one place their entire lives; some fly, some walk, many crawl. Life consists of a kaleidoscope of colors, body forms, body movements, digestive systems, sense organs, and other factors in endless diversity and combinations.

Besides the individual, the most basic grouping of life is the species. Typically, each species specializes in its own environment, with its own specific means of survival. Each has its own characteristics, and each can interbreed to produce fertile offspring only within the genetic boundaries of that species. In the rare cases where different species can successfully interbreed, the species are always closely related, and the offspring are sterile (as with mules, the offspring of horses and donkeys). But why these barriers, and why such diversity? In understanding this, we can begin to understand our development and evolution.

Only in the past 150 years have we really begun to understand what species are, and why they exist. Consider the situation in which a type of plant growing in a particular area slowly adapts to its external environment over the course of many generations. Now, suppose there's an instance of tectonic activity, and a mountain range arises in the middle of this landscape—not an uncommon occurrence in the history of life on Earth. The plant population is split into two. One side of the mountain chain may have more rainfall and sunlight than the other, so the plant population on that side will follow its own evolutionary path favoring hot, wet conditions. The other half of the population may lie in a region of little rain and sun, and will follow its own evolutionary path favoring cooler, dryer conditions.

Given a long enough period of separation, the two plant populations will no longer be interfertile; that is, crosses will no longer be able to produce fertile offspring, if they produce offspring at all. There will also be observable changes. After a thousand years, the two populations may look slightly different. Given another 100,000 years, they may look completely different. Each has specialized to fit its new environment, and the changes have become so extensive that the genes can no longer match up properly. While they have a common ancestor, the two species are now completely separate.

The tremendous age of our planet and the many tectonic and climatic changes that have resulted during that period caused split after split, after which separated populations of animals and plants continued along their separate genetic paths, which branched off again and again, resulting in the multitude of species we see today. Along the way, some species failed and became extinct; given enough time, almost all do. Often, the common ancestor to related species lies so far back in time that little or no evidence of it remains—except perhaps a fossil or two, if the plant or animal had hard parts, or died in an especially preservative environment.

It's possible to depict the different varieties of life as branches and leaves on a tree, with the different branches showing the splits between species and types. Using our knowledge of DNA and the fossil evidence, we have been able to construct a Giant Tree of Life, all stemming from those first few microbes.

Phylogenetic Tree of Life

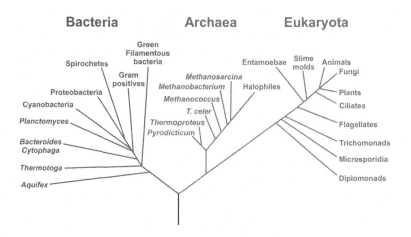

Figure 10: The classic Tree of Life, showing the development of life and the early separation of Bacteria, Archaea, and Eukaryotes.

What mechanism drives evolution? As I've already intimated, life adapts to the conditions it finds itself in—or dies out. Charles Darwin was the first to propose that existing species descended from common ancestry as a result of natural selection. Natural selection is the process by which certain traits with advantages over others allow certain individuals in a population to reproduce more successfully than others.

In time, their descendants outnumber all others, and the trait is spread throughout the entire species. If a new predator is faster than the others, and preys (for example) on deer, then all the slower deer will be caught and killed over time. The slow ones won't produce as many offspring as the fast ones before they die. Eventually, the entire deer population will become noticeable faster than their ancestors. In this case, natural selection has weeded out the genes for slowness.

Humans have observed many recent examples of natural selection in action. One of the most famous examples is the tiny peppered moth of England. Originally, the majority of peppered moths were light in color, to camouflage themselves against the light-colored trees and lichens they were resting on. However, with the advent of the Industrial Revolution, most of the lichens died out and the trees became blackened by soot. The paler moths were no longer camouflaged, and became easy prey for birds. But natural selection came into play, and within a few decades most of the peppered moth population was dark-colored. The white moths were caught and consumed in higher numbers than the black, whereas those darker in color survived to reproduce. The light-colored genes became dormant, and the dark-colored genes dominant.

Now that the English landscape is no longer covered with soot, the process seems to be reversing itself.

Now our list of evidence for evolution includes:

1. The presence of fossils in sequential geological layers, from simple life to the more complex.
2. Similar bodily structures in living organisms.
3. The presence of redundant body parts.
4. The sequence of embryonic development.
5. The distribution of species across the Earth.
6. The phylogenetic Tree of Life
7. Natural selection

Our understanding of the genetic basis of natural selection has become one of humanity's greatest discoveries; it is the grand Story of Life, and how we came about. The first evidence was discovered by the monk Gregor Mendel, who undertook a long series of experiments with peas at his monastery. Mendel noticed that certain characteristics in many species are passed on from parents to offspring. He wanted to understand how this happens; so for his experiments he chose to use pea plants, which are easy to grow, have short generations, and bear distinct characteristics. He chose seeds having seven clear characteristics. These included, among other things:

- Rounded and wrinkled seed shapes.
- Yellow and green seed colors.
- Green and yellow pods.

One might expect that by crossing plants with green and yellow pods, the result would be a plant with yellow-green pods. However, the results are more clear-cut and startling. Mendel's experiment showed that a cross between a plant with green pods and another with yellow pods produces *only* green pods in the first generation. However, yellow pods appear in roughly one-quarter of second generation plants.

Ultimately, Mendel came to the following conclusions: Each specific characteristic of the pea plants is a unit that is passed on to the offspring. In other words, a plant with pure green pods passes a green pod unit to all its seeds, and a plant with pure yellow pods only passes a yellow pod unit. If we cross-fertilize pea plants with green pods with pea plants with yellow pods, the new seeds receive both a yellow unit and a green unit for pod color. However, the green unit is stronger (more dominant) than the yellow unit, and as such the new seed, although having both green and yellow pod units, produces a plant with green pods. If this new plant is cross-fertilized with another plant of the same type (i.e., one that also contains green and yellow pod units) either parent can pass on either a green or yellow pod unit to its offspring, but not both. In the second generation, plants bearing yellow pods occur only in cases in which both parents happened to pass on a yellow pod unit, which occurs 25% of the time.

Today we understand these "units" to be genes. Genes always come in pairs, one inherited from each parent. For example, I have blue eyes, since I received a blue-eye gene from my mother and a blue-eye gene from my father. If I marry someone with brown eyes, my children will get a blue-eye gene from me, and a brown-eye gene from my wife. The brown-eye gene is dominant; so assuming my wife has two brown-eye genes, although my child have both blue and brown-eye genes, their eyes will be brown.

With the exception of prions and viruses (which may be only quasi-living), all living organisms are made up of cells, and within these cells we find a nucleus that contains stringy, helical fibers consisting of chemical bonds making liberal use of the common elements carbon, hydrogen, nitrogen, oxygen, sulfur, and phosphorus. This chemical is called deoxyribonucleic acid, or DNA; these stringy fibers themselves are known as chromosomes. Basically, chromosomes are chains of genes that contain the instructions to make proteins. These proteins are the building blocks for our hair, eyes, blood, and everything else in our bodies. These building instructions, the genes, come with variations called **alleles**. We all have similar genes for hair color, for example, but our genes are not exactly the same; and so my gene combination makes my hair brown, while another person's might make her hair black.

Every person has two copies of each gene, one inherited from each parent; and humans are estimated to have 20,000-25,000 gene pairs that decide how we will look, some of our behavior, our athletic ability, etc. No one carries the entire gene pool for humanity; a gene pool is the total number of all the genes and combinations of genes that can occur in a species. The bigger the gene pool and the greater the variety, the better the opportunity for adaptation to occur as environmental conditions change. As we've seen with the peppered moth, the presence of a recessive dark-coloring gene ensured its success during the sooty days of the Industrial Revolution; and later, the presence of a surviving light-coloring gene in the peppered moth gene pool served the species well as England became cleaner again.

The overall human population (nearly 7 billion individuals as of this writing) abounds with different genes and gene combinations. These genes result in some of us having a small build, while others are tall or fast, some are aggressive, some are good with their hands, and others can produce exquisite art. We all belong to the same species, but at the individual level there are subtle differences caused by the specific genes we carry.

Farmers have been practicing gene selection on their crops and domestic animals for millennia, though this represents artificial rather than natural selection. The farmer planting corn would use only the seeds of those plants that produced lush foliage and larger cobs for the next year's planting, unknowingly selecting for the genes that produced those characteristics. This helped those genes become predominant in the species. Eventually, the genes for small cobs were eliminated from the gene pool altogether. Practices like these were how our ancestors, without knowing it, slowly domesticated wild seed to produce today's crops, and how the wolf morphed into the dog—because people selected pups with specific traits to raise and breed.

Today we can observe rapid evolution in microbial life in response to our use of antibiotics. Antibiotics are used to kill harmful bacteria, and have become very important weapons in our medical arsenal. But some antibiotics such as penicillin have become much less effective than they originally were, as specific bacteria have evolved over thousands of their very short generations to become resistant to those antibiotics. An antibiotic may kill 99.99% of all bacteria, but if just one bacterium in 10,000 has undergone a random gene mutation to make it resistant to the antibiotic, it will survive to reproduce successfully, as will its descendants. Eventually, all individuals of that bacterial species will be resistant to the antibiotic. Survival of the fittest has created a new strain of the particular bacteria.

Since we now have the ability to analyze the DNA and genes of all organisms, we can make several conclusions. The first is that all living organisms do, in fact, have DNA and genes. All—including bacteria, flies, trees, lions, and humans—use the same basic building blocks. In fact, a large portion of an organism's DNA is identical to that in every other creature on Earth, no matter what kind of organism is examined. This demonstrates conclusively that all living species derived from a common origin. Life started out very simple, then developed and branched out into the various life forms we see today. Even if this seems improbable to you, remember the incredible time depth life has enjoyed to allow the improbable to occur: approximately four *billion* years.

The major driving force behind gene change is mutation—random copying errors caused by a variety of factors, including exposure to radiation from the Sun and radioactive materials, exposure to certain chemicals, and mistakes during cell division. You have a gene that builds your hair in a specific way, but a tiny mutation in this gene as your cells reproduce can cause it to be built in a slightly different way—for example, so that it produces red hair. If your sperm or egg cells contain the mutation, it is passed on to the next generation. If the mutation is beneficial or at least neutral in outcome, it may soon become quite prevalent throughout the population. More often, however, mutations kill us or cause severe health problems.

One example of a dangerous mutation in humans is one that occurs on a gene that regulates the components of sweat, digestive juices, and mucus. The mutation results in Cystic Fibrosis, which, amongst other things, may clog up one's airways due to mucus build-up. Life for those having this mutated gene is painful, and they are besieged with health problems. It's not the fault of the poor victim, but rather the result of a random mutation. About one in 25 people of European descent carry one gene for Cystic Fibrosis. Somewhere in human history, many tens of thousands years ago, a mutation took place on this gene in the European population; it was passed on, and is now quite prevalent in the human gene pool.

Very rarely, a genetic mutation is beneficial. For example, it was a mutation that caused the peppered moth to have a gene for producing darker coloration in the first place. This gene spread slowly through the population as the moths interbred. Later, as it became easier for predators to see and prey on the lighter-colored moths, only the darker ones survived to reproduce. The lighter coloration still occurred occasionally, but became recessive, since white color translated to death before reproduction could occur. Now the light coloring is making a comeback as dark-colored moths become easier to see again.

In the event of a severe climate change to much colder weather, animals that just happen to have a mutated gene for longer fur or more body fat have a better chance of surviving and reproducing. As only these members of the species can easily survive, the whole population slowly evolves to have longer hair.

This also helps explains why our original plant populations, now growing on opposite sides of the mountain range, have evolved to be different from each other. For the plant on the dry side, a mutated gene produced a thick skin that provided an advantage in dry times, because it could retain moisture longer. Slowly, this entire population evolved to have thicker skins. The plants on the other side of the mountain had no need for this gene; but there was a gene mutation somewhere in the gene pool that enabled the roots of certain plants to survive in very wet conditions, and so the root systems of this plant population changed over time. The genetic differences between the two plant populations continued to accumulate—until the species split in two, forming another branching on the Tree of Life.

By using our knowledge that such branchings can and do occur, even in the modern world—and by looking closely at the DNA of different species, as well as the fossil record—we can sometimes work our way backward in time to identify the nearest common ancestor of any two species. Science now knows how life evolved on the Earth. It is a process of random mutation that produces new traits in a species; if these traits are beneficial or neutral, they're passed on and may become dominant. There was no sudden creation of man and all the world's animals, and the DNA tells us this. If anything, creation is continuous, and there is no reason to credit a god with this effect.

But what else can we find if we take a closer look at DNA and genes? Can we find more clues to our evolutionary development? Can we find genes shared by all species, or genes that are still present in our DNA but no longer serving any purpose? Indeed we can, and this is yet another proof of our accidental evolutionary origins.

In 2003, the human genome was fully mapped. We began a search for the species closest to us, comparing our DNA to other animals'.

Comparisons revealed the chimpanzee to be humanity's closest living relative, with more than 94% of the DNA between the two species being identical (and by some estimates, more than 97%). This comes as no surprise to anyone who has seriously studied the comparative physiology. We now estimate that our common ancestor existed about 7 million years ago, whereupon the first human ancestor (probably the genus *Australopithecus)* went down one evolutionary path, and ancestral chimps went down another.

One example of a gene shared by chimpanzees and humans is the one that provides the blueprint for the protein molecule cytochrome C, which allows respiration within cells. It is a complicated molecule consisting of 104 amino acids that must occur in a very specific order to work properly. We find the exact same protein molecule in both the chimpanzee and human. If we examine the rhesus monkey, which is farther away from the human species in the Tree of Life, the cytochrome C molecule differs by one amino acid. For a horse, the difference is 11 amino acids; and for a tuna, 21 additional amino acids.

This begs a question: if we can do this, can work our way back through our DNA to the first common ancestor of all life on Earth? Is there something still remaining of that very ancient ancestor? And yes, we do find its remains in our DNA. The process by which information contained in the nuclear DNA is passed on to proteins is the same for all organisms. A process that evolved in the first living organisms billions of years ago is still being used, and is common to all living things—whether microbe, plant, fish, bird, mammal, or human. Other common processes are those used to produce energy and cell components.

We also know that many of our existing genes are inactive, at least as far as we can tell. Indeed, up to 50% of human genome can be considered "junk DNA" or "introns," as they do nothing but interrupt the protein-coding process. Some may be "periods" to tell a certain process when to stop. However, some are pseudogenes, which are genes that performed some function in our ancient past but no longer code for anything. For example, we humans have the almost-complete remains of a gene that manufactures Vitamin C. The gene is there, but is dysfunctional as it exists. If it worked, our species would never again have to worry about vitamin C deficiency—a.k.a. scurvy, a problem sailors often suffered until it was realized that a few citrus fruits now and then could prevent the illness, which can be fatal. Hence the term "Limeys" for British sailors.

The dysfunctional Vitamin C gene is common to all primates, the evolutionary line from which humans spring. It seems that about 63 million years ago, the coding broke down due to a mutation in a common ancestor—and the gene's ability was lost to all its descendants, including us. The loss may have occurred in response to a diet rich in vitamin C, which made the requirement for the gene obsolete. When the mutation occurred, its results did not matter; so the issue never got "fixed" by evolution.

Similarly, in dolphins we find genes allowing them to use their sense of smell, but those genes are no longer active. Some distant cetacean ancestor probably lost the gene's function, which didn't matter because the sense went mostly unused in the ocean.

Within the cells of all living organisms (except bacteria and Archaea) we also find subunits called mitochondria. The mitochondria fulfill an important role by generating energy for the cell to use. They are unique in that they have their own DNA, different from that of the parent organism; the mitochondria almost seem to be foreign bodies contained within the cell, and in fact that may be their evolutionary origin. There is strong evidence that during early life on Earth, the mitochondria were absorbed into simple, free-living cells. Since the mitochondria provided energy for the cells, the mitochondria and the cells that had tried to eat them developed a symbiosis that continues to this day.

Mitochondrial DNA is inherited only from one's mother, and it's very slow to change. But we do see mutations in the mitochondrial code; and when such a mutation occurs, it is passed on and spreads through the population if it's either neutral or beneficial. We can therefore take two living persons and analyze their mitochondrial DNA in order to determine how closely they are related. If it's exactly the same, then sometime in the relatively recent past they have a common female ancestor. By looking for particular mutations in mitochondrial DNA, it's possible to divide people into groups having common ancestral "mothers." Mitochondrial DNA mutations appear to occur in forms that can be passed on approximately once per 3,500 years.

Using this information, it has been calculated that all modern humans descend from a "Mitochondrial Eve" who lived about 200,000 years ago. Now, please note that this does *not* mean that there was only one human female alive 200,000 years ago; our common human ancestor was simply the one whose genetic viability was strongest and therefore won the "genetic war" to control the human genome. Ultimately, only her descendants survived and dominated.

We can now add more evidence for evolution, so that our list includes:

1. The presence of fossils in sequential geological layers, from simple life to the more complex.
2. Similar bodily structures in living organisms.
3. The presence of redundant body parts.
4. The sequence of embryonic development.
5. The distribution of species across the Earth.
6. The Phylogenetic Tree of Life.
7. Natural selection.
8. DNA presence and structure in all living organism

Today we understand the mechanism of evolution very well, and we can even reproduce it in our laboratories. But where did the first life begin—those original bits of biology?

The oldest fossils that we have found so far are those of prokaryotes (cyanobacteria), which are cellular organisms without a membrane-enclosed nucleus. In Western Australia we find fossilized structures called stromatolites where cyanobacteria cemented sedimentary grains together as far back as 3.45 billion years ago—not long after the Earth cooled sufficiently for life as we know it to take hold. It was an astonishing and remarkable event, in which inorganic compounds formed organic, carbon-based bonds that later developed the ability to self-replicate. Once these very basic life forms had the ability to replicate, random mutations ensured their evolution to higher forms of life. Again, the remains of these first building blocks are still present in *all* living organisms.

In 1952, Stanley Miller and Harold Urey performed the first experiment to test the possibility of life forming under the conditions of the early Earth's atmosphere. They used methane, water, ammonia, and hydrogen sealed in a sterile, closed system. The water was heated up enough to evaporate, and sparks were induced inside the system to simulate lightning. Within a week, 10-15% of the carbon in the system had been converted into organic compounds, with 2% forming several amino acids, the building blocks of DNA. While the Miller/Urey experiments have since been criticized, mostly because we suspect the Earth's ancient atmosphere may have been quite different than Miller and Urey speculated, the composition and conditions present on primitive Earth must have been conductive to forming organic compounds from inorganic substances—compounds that are the building blocks of today's life.

In this ancient broth of amino acids, the first nucleotides (five-carbon sugars) formed. It is postulated that these free-floating molecules floated in a warm sea or other accommodating environment, where they regularly bonded to each other to form longer molecules. These chains were to become the first primitive forms of life, and may have resembled the modern viruses that take the form of a single strand of RNA. Millions of different bonds must have formed, just to be broken up again. Only some survived more than a few minutes or hours. Somewhere on the primordial Earth, some of these nucleotide chains survived by forming or finding themselves within a protective bubble. These may have been the bubbles on a seashore, where fatty acids formed a thin layer of protection. This isolated them from undergoing further chemical interactions, therefore holding off destruction by the hostile world outside. The membrane and RNA found a mutual benefit in each other, as the RNA fed the membrane and helped it stay intact.

Those RNA chains not having a bubble to protect them, or that were unable to sustain the membrane, simply broke up. In the course of time, the protected RNA found a way to copy itself, as another strand of RNA built around the existing strand. Then the membrane split, each containing a copy of the RNA. Because this new RNA had the ability to survive and replicate, it soon became the dominant molecule in its particular soup of amino acids and nucleotides.

RNA also helped to bond amino acids together, the first step to forming proteins. The stage was set for the development of the first proto-cell. For the next one billion years or so, the Earth's oceans teemed with these primitive life forms as they slowly evolved further. The RNA soon got displaced by DNA, the familiar double-helix, perhaps when a replicating RNA strand failed to "unzip" and pull apart once the child strand was completed. Whatever the case, DNA is much more stable than the RNA—though RNA still performs vital actions in all living organisms. During the next billion years, the first complex single-celled organisms, eukaryotes—which possess a membrane-bound nucleus and chromosomes—evolved. Once sexual reproduction got underway, allowing two organisms to swap their genetic material, evolution took off as random mutations increased the variety of the genetic material. The characteristics that allowed an organism to better adapt to its environmental conditions were preserved by natural selection. The timeline for the development of life, based on our current knowledge, is as so:

1. The first RNA/DNA contained in a membrane appeared. This development happened within the first billion years after the Earth cooled off.

2. It took 1-2 billion years to form the first complex single-celled organisms (eukaryotes).

3. Eukaryotes became dominant and widespread. As they produced oxygen, the atmosphere became oxygen-rich. We see the evidence in our iron mines. The earliest iron beds contain no iron oxide, which forms when iron reacts with oxygen. Only in layers younger than 2.3 billion years do we find iron oxide.

4. Once enough oxygen built up in the atmosphere, it became conducive to aerobic life, which accelerated development.

5. Collagen (fine strands of fiber holding cells together) developed. Cells started sticking to each other. The first primitive cell colonies appeared. Collagen still binds multicellular organisms together today.

6. The earliest multicellular creatures evolved further and became larger. Some parts of the body started to become specialized. Eventually, some of these basic life forms began moving deliberately by compressing the body and releasing it again. They could now travel in search of food.

7. At some point, bilateral symmetry evolved, and in one lineage, a head and tail developed. The first primitive light-sensitive cells formed in the head as a precursor to eyes. Claws and legs also started to develop in some creatures, producing most of the common body designs known today.

8. Sexual reproduction took hold. As genetic material was swapped, evolution accelerated. The earliest sexual reproduction may have been similar to the way corals reproduce today. Once a year, at exactly the same time, all the corals release clouds of sperm and egg-cells. These recombine to form new coral organisms.

9. The Cambrian Explosion took place about 570 million years ago. Evolution accelerated by at least an order of magnitude, The diversity of life today stems from this time period; it ultimately resulted in primates, one lineage of which was to evolved into the human race.

Where Humans Came From

So few of us know much about evolution. Often, primary and secondary schools are discouraged from teaching or simply not allowed to teach evolution, due to pressure from religious groups. However, evolution has become almost universally accepted in the scientific community, as it best explains life's origins and development as recorded in the physical and biological sciences. While the details are still being debated, few scientists in any field question the basic concept of evolution.

Meanwhile, none of the current religious establishments have been able to absorb this knowledge into their teachings. After all, evolution is a stark contrast to the sudden creation of man and the Earth by a god—and scientists are willing to question and fine-tune knowledge to better fit their observations, rather than forcing their observations to fit a foregone conclusion and then ignoring any that do not.

Human Development

The evolution of life on Earth ultimately produced the species *Homo sapiens sapiens*—us. The evolution of our species is a magnificent development, a witness to the powerful outcome of random genetic mutation and the natural selection of the appropriate traits to ensure survival of the fittest.

Our children should no longer be taught magical fables about how humanity came into being. Instead, we can tell them the fascinating true tale of the creation of the Earth, from stellar nebula to the molten rock that eventually cooled to form a barren world—a place where the first seeds of life formed from primordial chemicals that started to multiply and evolve on their own, leading to today's incredible biodiversity billions of years later. We can tell them about the fossilized footsteps that have been found on the shores of an ancient African lake, where two proto-humans walked in volcanic ash more than 1.6 million years ago.

To find the roots of our own species, we need to go back more than 60 million years ago, when the first primates evolved. They were small animals, squirrel-like in size but with feet increasingly adapted for grasping (probably so they could hold onto tree limbs better). They also had binocular vision, with eyes set in the front of the face so their visual fields overlapped, proving better depth perception as they hunted for bugs and fruit. From these early primates the first monkeys developed, appearing as early as 33 million years ago. Compared to primates, they had fewer teeth, less prominent snouts, larger brains, and increasingly forward-looking eyes.

New selective pressures were exerted on these proto-monkeys, especially when tropical forests were replaced by grasslands and shrub
lands due to climate change. Some species adapted to (mostly) living
on the ground. The ancestors of the great apes branched off the monkey family tree about 30 million years ago. Several ape lineages developed, and 14 million years ago, the group of African apes that would
ultimately develop into our ancestors was established.

The increasingly colder climates caused many primate species to
become extinct. About 9 million years ago, one of the ape species diverged into two lines: namely the gorillas, and the line that would
eventually lead to humans and chimpanzees. Below is a schematic
time-line of our development.

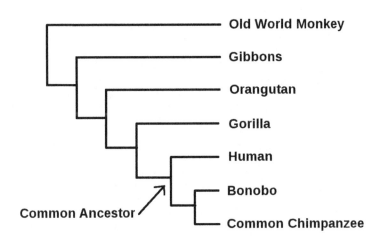

Figure 11: The divergence of humans and great apes
from a common ancestor

The open, grassy plains favored the evolution of novel adaptations
to reach food, observe predators, and to otherwise survive in the ever-
shrinking African forests. One change set our species apart. One of
the great ape species began to spend more and more time standing

upright. Was it because of a quest to reach for fruit on higher tree limbs, or simply to see across the plains? Both? Whatever the reason, it clearly provided an evolutionary advantage to that species, as its bone structure, especially the pelvis and hip bones, evolved to support bipedalism (that is, standing and walking on two feet). Modern humans can easily stand upright for hours, with little effort, simply by resting on this evolved bone structure. These skeletal changes help paleontologists distinguish between ape and human fossils.

The use of the hind legs as a primary means to move around also had a secondary effect: the front legs were freed for other uses, and could be used to manipulate objects and use tools. Their grasping structure made this even easier.

We can see the evolution of these traits in human fossil collections. One of the most remarkable fossil hominids (i.e., proto-human and human species) that paleontologists have found is that of the species *Australopithecus afarensis.* Dating to about 3.2 million years old, she stood just 1.1 meters (3.5 feet) tall. Her gait was less perfect than ours, and she may have walked bent over, but she was definitely bipedal.

We have also discovered footsteps of our ancient ancestors. In 1976, paleontologist Mary Leakey unearthed the fossilized footprints of three individuals who walked at a leisurely pace through moist volcanic ash more than 3.5 million years ago. The footprints were quickly covered up and preserved as the ash hardened. The footsteps showed that the upright walking stance and the human foot had already evolved by then.

After their evolutionary split from the ape family, the hominids developed further. Based on our current knowledge, between 12 and 19 different species and subspecies evolved in two genuses: *Australopithecus* ("southern ape-man") and *Homo* ("human"). All of them are now extinct, apart from our own species, *Homo sapiens sapiens.* Apparently the last hominids that we shared the planet with were the Neanderthals, who may have been an "archaic" subspecies of *Homo sapiens* rather than a separate species of humans. Neanderthals became extinct as recently as 25,000 years ago, possibly being forced to extinction by our doings. It's also possible that the disputed species *H. floresiensis,* a.k.a. Flores Man or "hobbits," may have died out on the Indonesian island of Flores as recently as 12,000-13,000 years ago.

Figure 12: Reconstruction of a female Australopithecus afarensis

Our own species may have evolved as far back as 250,000 years ago. Our large brains and increased tool usage sets us apart from other hominids (although it has to be noted that Neanderthals had even larger brains, and also produced advanced stone tools). We all have remarkably homogenous DNA, showing evidence of a human evolutionary "bottleneck" fairly recently in geological terms. This probably resulted from some cataclysmic event, such as an ice age or widespread volcanism, that reduced our species to a very small population, from which it then expanded again. That population may have been as small as a few thousand. Some 70,000 to 50,000 years ago, small groups of anatomically modern humans started moving out of Africa, and new and distinctive genetic characteristics developed in isolated groups. Today we can trace back every individual to a specific world region from which his or her ancestors originated. The DNA of a given race, e.g. Asian, is also very homogeneous. The San people in southern Africa have the most diverse DNA, indicating the great age of that population and suggesting that they're the direct descendants of our post-bottleneck founding population.

The story of humanity, then, is the story of the evolution of first the mammal and later the primate lineages, both of which ultimately originated from that first small cell which formed in an ancient sea billions of years ago. The evidence for evolution is overwhelming. There was no instant creation of man, no Great Architect with a blueprint in his hand.

In the next section we'll look at how we function and define ourselves. Only then we will be able to define our future in the context of a new framework replacing current religions.

This Species Called Humans

From the evidence we've gathered from the physical world around us (especially during the past 100 years), everything points to our having evolved to our current state over billions of years, from the first basic life forms to the species we are today. The animal brain, which initially contained only a few basic light sensors and nerves to encode and react to light, became highly developed during those eons. It became so advanced, in fact, that in the last 200,000 years or so, hominids evolved high intelligence and developed a sense of self-awareness. In recent centuries, we've even begun to understand the processes and mechanisms responsible for our development.

Where previously we were merely being pushed ahead on the evolutionary conveyor belt, if you will, we are now increasingly taking control of our environment. We routinely tinker with life, breeding for specific traits and, in the last few decades, have begun to directly manipulate genes. We can influence the weather and climate.

Electromagnetism is no longer a mystery, and is now used for everything from lighting to communication, entertainment, and industrial processes. We have learned how to harness nuclear energy, and can destroy all life on the planet if we wish to. In a sense, we have become gods ourselves. In these terms, *Homo sapiens sapiens* has become the most advanced and dominant form of life on Earth—yet only in the past few centuries have we begun to systematically and routinely understand ourselves as a part of nature.

As we prepare to escape the shackles of our ancient religions, it's important that we understand how we function, behave, and think. What *is* this species called *Homo sapiens sapiens?* Knowing more about ourselves will enable us to define a better model and future for our descendants.

Looking around us, we very quickly notice that we are all quite different, despite the fact that we belong to the same species and share a close physical similarity. We all have our own personality traits (something we'll explore further in a later section). Our levels of intelligence and ways of responding to the world differ. As parents we are often surprised by how different our children are from us. Some are sociable and laugh easily; others are more quiet or sullen. Some get angry quickly, while others are patient and good-natured. Some are good at music and art; some are better in math. But why the differences, and how do we become the "me" that each of us is?

Clearly, if inherited traits form the building blocks of a personality, then the external world and internal reasoning must mold the final shape of the personality and belief system of each individual. The best place to start to understand personality, then, is with a newborn child who has yet to discover the world.

A child goes through different stages of physical and mental development to become the "me," or "soul" as defined by most religions. A child's first six years are critical in the development and behavior of the later adult, and are predominantly shaped by the following factors:

1. Basic genetic personality traits;
2. The caregiver(s), e.g. parents or nanny;

3. Social interaction with family and friends;
4. The child's internal interpretation and analysis of the external world.

It comes as no surprise that a child's caregivers have a major influence on the later adult, and there are no relationships more important than the first attachments the child forms. Pity the child born in a world with little love, warmth, or understanding. Driven by an internal longing for acceptance, the child is rejected, ignored, or even abused from the start. The self-image and mental development of the child suffers a severe onslaught, and he or she develops feelings of not being good enough, shame, and defensiveness, which result in low self-esteem, unhappiness, and depression.

An intimate, warm relationship between infant and parent/caregiver results in the healthy mental development of the child. Forming an attachment with a sensitive, responsive adult enables the child to feel secure in exploring the world. Studies have pointed out that in those cases where a secure attachment between an adult and infant is present, the child develops proper social skills, intellect, and formation of a social identity. A well-studied case of an institution with 45 infants under 18 months old, cared for by only six nurses with minimal contact, showed the infants to fall severely behind in their development, coupled with serious personality deficiencies.

The stage is set with the type of attachments the child forms—and again this is the first major and lasting influence on the child. When the child finds himself in an adult world, his yet-unformed brain must interpret and take cues from those around him. The feedback provided and boundaries set by his/her caregivers play a major role in this process. A child may be brought up under one of four primary parenting styles:

- **Authoritarian Parenting:** In this parenting style, the parents set strict rules and the children are expected to follow them without question. Disobedience results in punishment, and there is little (if any) room for discussion. These parents do not explain to the child their reasons for being punished. Disobedience or questioning is seen as a challenge to their authority. Mostly these children are obedient and capable, but test lower in happiness, social competence, and self-esteem.

- **Authoritative Parenting:** These parents firmly and consistently enforce clear limits to their children's behavior. However, they listen and are responsive to the questions of these children. Disciplinary actions are undertaken to support and guide the child rather than to punish him. Reasons are given for the punishment. These parents show acceptance, empathy, and support for their kids. Reason prevails over authoritarian rules. These kids overall have high self-esteem, show higher levels of happiness, and are generally more mentally healthy and successful.

- **Permissive parenting:** These parents rarely discipline their children. They may show love and affection, but set no limits on behavior. They make few demands on their children and avoid confrontation. They are sometimes more a friend than a parent. The child is in control of the relationship. Generally, these children measure low on happiness and the capability of doing things for themselves. They often perform poorly at school, have difficulty adjusting socially, and experience problems with authority.

- **Uninvolved Parenting:** The child's basic needs are fulfilled, but there is a lack of support and communication with the child. The child has no one to turn to, and is offered little or no affection and support. The parents have little insight on the child's life and live separate lives from their child. Overall, these children have a low self-esteem and are not as competent as their peers.

There are exceptions to the above parenting methods, of course, not to mention how the children involved react to them. Some children have an innate resilience, and despite their external circumstances can persevere to become successful, happy adults. As the child grows older, he begins to interact with his peers (other children), and they further shape and influence his personality. Whereas in the family he has taken on a certain position and role, it disappears or evolves as the child finds himself in a playgroup or in the company of other kids. Within this group the child is no longer distinguished as a family member, but finds himself roughly equal to his peers.

The child must find recognition and acceptance for himself in the group; no one is going to do it for him. The internal drive for acceptance and validation as an individual drives him to find friends and to be accepted by them. The child must be alert not to be ridiculed or teased. The child must also win the praise and affection of the supervising adult, and (eventually) find acceptance with the opposite sex. The feedback he receives from the playgroup is used by the child to form an opinion of himself, and it further molds and shapes his personality.

For example, a child of Chinese immigrants in the USA will conform to the American school group. The child will take on the speech patterns, thinking, and norms of the school group despite the very different culture waiting for him at home. This, then, becomes the second major influence on the child.

Thirdly— and this is where the child's beliefs, morals and view of the world develop—is the process of internalization. The child takes his experience of the world and the guidance he receives and, using internal reasoning, constructs his own framework and philosophy to guide how he behaves, believes, and think. We all have within us moral standards that we set for ourselves, an internal form of guidance. So strong is this moral framework that we will sometimes forsake ourselves for its sake.

In many cases, internalization is the result of accepting norms provided by the examples of influential figures or role models. The process starts with learning a norm, and then the child goes through the process of analyzing and arguing about it and its value internally. Finally, the child adopts it, and it becomes integrated into the internal philosophy/framework that guides his actions. The norm is now set.

Religions aim to set their norms and values using the same process.

Although some religious norms thus learned are well-intended , the package of irrational beliefs that often come with any religious norm makes it into a blunt tool for smashing through arguments, both internal and external, and destroying the rights and beliefs of others.

We also develop our personalities and behavior in response to the groups we find ourselves with. Judith Rich Harris has proposed three mechanisms for socialization and personality development in young people, namely:

- Forming and maintaining beneficial relationships (the Relationship System)
- Becoming and remaining an accepted member of a group (the Socialization System)
- Competing successfully with one's rivals (the Status System)

In the Relationship System, we keep collecting information and judgments about individual people we meet or interact with. Evolution equipped us well with this mechanism, because if we are to survive, we had better know who we're dealing with. Ultimately, our relationships take up a large part of our thinking and behavior.

In the Socialization System, we collect information on specific categories of people. One of our strengths as a species is our sense of belonging. Few of us can function entirely alone. Loneliness brings unhappiness, whereas a group provides social support and a sense of belonging—whether it's a church group, a Boy Scouts troop, or a chess club. A group also attaches norms and rules to behavior. Socialization is an extremely attractive process, and a child will typically conform to the social behavior of his peers. Again, evolution has forced us to make sure we're accepted, because those without a group are ridiculed, marginalized, and deprived of protection—so they quickly perish, often without reproducing. The message here is, socialize or suffer!

In the Status System, we compare ourselves to those around us. We find ourselves a niche in a group where we're not dominated by others. We adapt ourselves as we jostle for position. The girl who feels prettier may become more extroverted and confident that as such she has the attention of others. Our behaviors evolve in line with our status and drive for status.

Moral Development

As our personalities crystallize, moral development also takes place. But what *are* morals, exactly—and who determines what's right or wrong? Religions usually claim exclusive ownership of morality, arranging things so that only religion can ensure and set moral values. They appoint themselves our moral watchdogs. Religions, however, almost always offer crude, ancient models of moral behavior, based on a few historic individuals who made up the rules according to their own beliefs, culture, and technical knowledge. The morals and laws of Moses offer a good example of this; today, they often seem less than moral, especially after a reading of Numbers, Leviticus, and other books of the Old Testament text. Indeed, some of Moses' actions seem evil according to today's standards.

These days we know much more about the world, but we still live under the shadow of these ancient, imperfect morals.

Morality begins developing at birth, and is mostly determined by a child's caregivers and the social rules of the community he finds himself in. Lawrence Kohlberg grouped moral development into three levels. In Pre-Conventional Morality, which takes place during a child's early years, he sees rules as fixed and uses external feedback (pain, scolding, reward) as a source of understanding and interpreting the expected morals. The child then develops and starts to see other viewpoints, and starts to reason about these. In the second stage, Conventional Morality, children or young adults see morals as a way to behave well, function in a society, and meet the approval of their family and peers. This further evolves into regarding one's cultural morals as the natural way for a society to function. With Post-Conventional Morality, the person realizes that moral standards are subjective, and that there is no absolute right or wrong. Morals are agreed upon by a society to ensure its continued functioning, and sometimes the person even evaluates different moral values, which better fit another society. He's also accepted and internalized his moral principles based on his own evaluation and reasoning, which may differ from the prevailing view of his society.

Many people never achieve this third stage, or if they do, may backslide into the previous one.

It is therefore no surprise that we see variations between moral value sets from culture to culture. One culture may frown on nudity, whereas another is more open to it. In extreme cases, we may find very unusual cultural values, as in a child soldier in Burundi participating in killings. His social and moral world does not see anything wrong with this behavior; indeed, it encourages and approves such behavior.

Of course, there are a few universal human morals which we find in *almost* every culture, as they enable us to coexist with others: proscriptions against murder and incest, for example. Unfortunately, we do have psychologically disturbed individuals who break these moral laws, after which society quickly punishes them or removes them as a threat to society as a whole.

Morals are human-made; nature does not and cannot care about morals. In nature, we may see a pack of lions devouring a buffalo alive, or killing the mother of young offspring with impunity.

The Roles We Take On

By the time a young adult leaves school, much of his personality has been formed, shaped by his genetic disposition, culture, caregivers, peer groups, and belief systems. By this time, young people in (for example) Pakistan and Germany already interpret their lives by means of vastly different frameworks. The next big transition for that individual is to adulthood. The personality shaped in their first few years is now ready to take its place as an adult. The new adult will probably soon become a caregiver himself, and will have to sustain himself and his family.

The countless variables involved—e.g., making friends, meeting a life partner, finding a job—set us all on different courses in life. The once-shy girl becomes a successful company executive; the lovely and popular girl ends up with an abusive husband. Meeting and hearing about one's old classmates is witness to the many paths we all take. Our paths and experiences shape us further as we undergo other transition points in life: having children, getting married, finding a new job, retiring.

We also take on various roles throughout life, following the particular norms and rules for the role. A woman may serve as mother to her children, in which role she is expected to be caring, soothing, and patient. She may also be a teacher, in which case she must be firm, decisive and sometimes stern. At night she may be a lover, whereupon she becomes sexy and flirtatious.

Similarly, an office manager may be known as being strict and fearsome at work, whereas his own mother sees him as a loving and caring young man.

It's no mean feat to stand strong and steadfast in the outside world. Every individual must find ways to negotiate the culture around him, always seeking (and hopefully finding) a sense of belonging, acceptance and purpose. The "I" is always in search of love and acceptance, to reaffirm himself. We all carry in ourselves the notion of an ideal self (the way we want to be) and the actual self. We keep evaluating ourselves, and if we fail ourselves, we may feel disappointed. Personally, I want to be someone who gets up early and does productive work. Sometimes I succeed and feel good about myself; other times I fail, and feel badly about myself.

Religion also sets expected behavior; and the believer is always engaged in a constant struggle between his actual self and the ideal model demanded by his religious beliefs. Since a god and the afterlife are involved, the struggle can become very painful and intensive, especially if some goals cannot easily (or ever) be attained. The believer may also find himself in a position where he fears that he may have missed something small, and will be punished by his god in response. Every step is weighed and checked, in case it is in violation of the ideal religious self.

Within this vast variety, we find so many different viewpoints and beliefs that they're all but uncountable. Some emerge as a result of the culture and society a person was born into; some he acquires from his caregivers, from reading books, from watching television, or from examining his internalized beliefs. One person may have internalized a desire to be frugal in his life; another may have internalized a desire never to hurt anyone. The world is awash with various and often conflicting convictions and beliefs. It's no surprise, then, that the history of the world is an almost unrelenting tapestry of conflict, often triggered by religious differences. We all have convictions or attitudes on almost every topic, ranging from politics and sex before marriage to how to raise a child and how this world came about.

We know that parents have a strong influence on their children's attitudes, if only because they convey their own attitudes using praise and reward for expected behavior. Children's attitudes mostly mirror those of their parents. Friends may also instill attitudes, and at times these may be strong enough to replace the parents'. This also explains the stranglehold of religion. Children of religious parents have the religious attitudes of their parents, and often they believe them regardless of the facts of the matter.

How do we go about solving this conundrum of people having different attitudes about the world? By all accounts, the best solution is for us to start using facts and reason to come to the most plausible explanations and convictions, without allowing our own emotions and prejudices to taint this process.

We need to reexamine the question of why we have the different personality traits we're born with in the first place. There is increasing evidence that existing personality traits developed as a result of our evolutionary past. Being an extrovert allows a person to socialize easily with and seek the company of others, a trait which (among other things) provides an individual a reproductive advantage. On the other hand, the trait of agreeableness (e.g., being compassionate and cooperative) helps a person become more accepted, leading to a greater likelihood of protection by the community, again ensuring their survival. Openness, intellect, and creativity can help a person find innovative and cunning ways to survive or win reproductive partners.

The human population abounds with these different personality traits, none of them so dominant as to delete the others. If every member of the population were considerate and cooperative, then the few cheaters would take ample advantage, to the detriment of everyone else. These cheaters would inevitably increase in number. Similarly, impulsiveness—which has its advantages in some individuals in some circumstances—might soon lead to the entire population's demise if everyone bore the trait, because they wouldn't take all the facts into account before making potentially dangerous decisions.

Ultimately, the personality traits present in human populations are expressions of genetic traits that had some kind of benefit for the survival of the population or species, as well as the individuals who initially bore them. Indeed, evolution has produced several basic personality types within the modern human race. Psychological researchers have broadly classified five categories, which can be revealed through the use of an extensive test in which the individual scores points on each type, with the highest score indicating his most dominant traits. Again, it must be emphasized that these are broad categories.

Personality Types

Human personalities exist in five broad domains: extraversion, agreeableness, conscientiousness, neuroticism, and openness. We all bear some of the five traits to some extent, with one being more dominant than the others.

1. **Extraversion** is a tendency to seek the company of and enjoy being with others. Extraverts are normally perceived as action-orientated and energetic. This includes characteristics such a being social and talkative, and expressing themselves emotionally.

2. **Agreeableness** includes compassion, cooperation, and the value of getting along with others. These people are seen as friendly and helpful, and may put the interests of others ahead of their own.

3. **Conscientiousness:** Those scoring high on this trait tend to be organized, and plan carefully rather than take impulsive actions. They are thoughtful and self-disciplined, with good self-control, and prefer to set goals.

4. **Neuroticism:** These persons may be controlled by negative emotions such as anxiety and depression. They may be easily

irritated and moody at times, and even emotional unstable. Challenges in life are perceived as negative.

5. **Openness:** People with this trait are open to new ideas and are intellectually curious. Imagination and insight test high in these individuals, and they may also appreciate art and beauty. They may hold unconventional ideas and be very creative.

Via evolutionary development, we have also developed a very keen and sensitive emotional detection system. In a crowd of faces, we can quickly identify an angry one. Upon finding ourselves in a group of people, we read those around us and adapt to their personality types. We seek reproductive partners based on their personality traits, and these then also very much determine our quality of life. The female who selects a partner low on conscientiousness may pay a price in terms of poor job performance and diminished income. The individual high on the agreeableness score will find himself easily accepted by a group or friends.

So much of our lives depend on our friendships, coalitions, and partnerships. We have developed a myriad of ways to survive. Some of us are kind and compassionate, to allow acceptance by the group as a survival strategy. Some of us are aggressive and abusive, as these traits can create a situation of dominance that, at some point, helped individuals survive. We also find personality traits among animals, as all of us with pets have observed. However, the higher the brain development of the species, the stronger the presence of personality traits.

The Last 100 Years of Ancient Religions

The knowledge we have accumulated in the past two hundred years has increasingly threatened our religious models—to the point where the current disparity between religions and science has become untenable, and a serious threat to religion. This has begun to greatly influence the religious landscape. People cope by 1) ignoring scientific facts in favor of their religious beliefs; 2) finding some understanding in themselves with an altered belief system; or 3) breaking their emotional attachment to a specific religion.

Where religion previously explained the creation of the world, science is now providing a better and more consistent understanding of how it came into being. Religion also previously explained and set human behavior; this is now being replaced with knowledge of how we humans work and why we act in certain ways. God was previously the ultimate rectifier for unjustness—i.e., He would punish the evil with Hell, and reward the righteous with Heaven. This theocracy is now being replaced by human legal systems, where acceptable human values are used to bring those in the wrong to justice.

The religious model can no longer sustain itself. Creaking along under ever-increasing scrutiny, it is bound to change or disappear in the next 100 years. The change is already underway. But we can take comfort in knowing that the evolution of our religions is nothing new. If we look back into our past we soon realize that religion is in flux, continuously changing and developing, and always has been.

We may have recently undergone a long period of relatively stable religious dogmas, but we are on the cusp of change. Remember our first religions, which our ancestors used to explain and understand the world around them via magic and animism. In these religions, rituals were used to make contact with the unseen world, and later to find favor with or to influence the material world. Many of our gods developed from these early ancient religions until they grew into the ominous, all-powerful deities so many believe in today. Parallel to these, other religious frameworks developed—e.g. Buddhism, Confucius, etc.

The transition to a post-religious world is already taking place, rocking traditional religion to its roots. Over the course of the next century, realistic beliefs about the universe, based on our knowledge and reason, will start replacing our ancient religions and their gods. Any remaining traces of religion will differ substantially in their dogma, as they will *have* to start incorporating our scientific knowledge or disappear altogether. A hundred years from now, our religion will change substantially, with the current religions diluted and the majority replaced with a new understanding of ourselves and the world.

The tension between the different religions, their inability to adequately explain the natural world, and our increasing understanding of how the cosmos and life function require us to change, to move beyond our mystic, ancient gods to a new and modern understanding of the world and ourselves. The gods, if they exist, can always appear physically to reclaim their human subjects. It is up to them!

But we have neither seen nor heard from these gods in the past 2,000 years at the very least; and any claims otherwise are nothing more than claims, entirely improvable. Our gods have never appeared to us and never will. We have fooled ourselves into creating and believing in them. It is time to propose and formulate the next stage of our spiritual and cultural development.

The New Non-Religious Framework

Using our current knowledge of the cosmos, the development of life, and our understanding of ourselves, a new culture framework can be proposed. Existing information tells us:

- The solar system was created 4.6 billion years ago when a cloud of dust and gas in outer space began to collapse, possibly due to the interaction of some sort of shock wave (possibly caused by a nova or supernova) and its own gravitation.
- Life started on Earth no later than 3.4 billion years ago. It was very simple life, which progressively became more complex using the mechanism of survival of the fittest.
- Our own species appeared no earlier than 200,000 years ago, one of many hominid species that appeared after about 4 million years ago.
- The universe is governed by predictable and discoverable laws of physics, chemistry, and other physical sciences.

Science does not yet know everything; nor does it pretend to, unlike religion. Included among the great mysteries are:

- Why and how the Cosmos came to exist in the first place.
- How the first basic life form came into existence.

We do have ideas about these mysteries; and again, it would be easy to fall back on the old explanation of a god being responsible for all of the above. However, the hypothesis of gods fails, as we cannot see or find them. We have no choice but to lay down the following for our new modern framework, based on what the overwhelming mass of evidence we have collected over the centuries tells us:

1. The human race is the result of unguided evolution, from the first basic life forms to the more complex. This process is still ongoing and is observable in nature.

2. We evolved to fit the conditions and physical laws prevailing in the cosmos; the conditions were not specifically set to allow our existence.

3. There are no supernatural gods. The world around us, and the cosmos beyond, evolved based on the results of interactions of physical laws.

4. There is *nothing* supernatural. Anything we cannot explain is ascribable to our inadequate knowledge at this point, and may be explained at a later time.

5. We define our own human purposes, without supernatural influence.

6. Knowledge is gained from scientific analysis, observation, and experimentation, not from contradictory sacred texts compiled by committee hundreds of years after the purported events they report on.

7. Human personality is a function of biology and chemistry. It forms through the interaction of inborn characteristics (via inherited genes) with a specific social setting.

8. Morals and values are manmade functions of society, designed to ensure we can live together in harmony.

9. There is no real evidence of an afterlife or soul. However it does not concern us. If there is an afterlife it will be available to all and accessible to all. One does not have to take on a specific belief or God to attain this

Needless to say, this is a radical departure from our existing religions and their perceptions of our purpose in life. There is no grand Plan, just the plan we each make for ourselves and our societies. There is no god standing by with superpowers to help us. Everything we accomplish we must accept credit or blame for. We stand revealed as small and exposed, as we now realize how lonely and small we are in this vast universe. Yet we are, nonetheless, freer as a result, better equipped for the future. We have become a torch of complex life in the vast universe—as far as we know, the only such torch—and this is the responsibility weighing heavy on our shoulders. If we lose what we have on Earth, complex life may be forever lost to the universe. With the myth of our gods exposed, we are psychologically and emotionally forced to find the meaning of life for ourselves.

We should no longer look for gods to give us purpose. That is now our sole responsibility, devolving all the way down to the individual level. It's up to each of us to decide how to give our lives meaning, and to learn how to live those lives sincerely and affectionately. The question is no longer "What is the meaning of life?" It is now "What is the meaning of *my* life?" The ego must, in each case, find ways to overcome the emotional pain and challenges that go with living. We must take responsibility for living this life, for finding personal fulfillment, for taking into cognizance those around us, and ultimately for aspiring to the greater good of life and humanity.

For above all else, humans are social animals, requiring others around them to find acceptance and confirmation.

The previous era of devotion and obedience to god is now being replaced by a notion of life, reason, knowledge, humanism, and science. We now place emphasis on our own well-beings, the well-being of humankind in general, life itself, and the advancement of knowledge and science. Opinions and beliefs are formed on the basis of science, logic, and reason, and ideally are not to be influenced by our emotions, irrational beliefs, or the supernatural. Nothing is truth unless proven by knowledge and reason.

We are awakening to the liberation of the human consciousness from the primitive, from ancient teachings based on illogic and ignorance. We are becoming human—the pinnacle of evolution, the true "sapient, sapient man" of our own scientific designation. We represent consciousness in the vast universe—perhaps the only such beacon there is. We already have the knowledge to change the world, for good or ill, in ways that the creators of the ancient gods never dreamed of.

We have become gods ourselves.

How will this change us? Let's take a look at a hypothetical person called Jim. Jim is representative of many of us: he has an average job, friends, and a family. In the times of the gods, Jim had the following beliefs: There is a god I need to serve, and also a book containing the rules of what is expected from me. Every now and then I go to a place where I find others believing in the same god. Together we listen to someone preach about our god and what is expected from us in order to live in accordance with my god.

Jim has colleagues who have other beliefs; he feels sorry for them, as he believes that they're on the wrong path. He has been taught that his god is the only true one. Jim also struggles to reconcile the scientific findings he's been made aware of with the way he's been taught. Jim is afraid of death, but he hopes that by pleasing his god and doing what is required from him, this god may grant him an afterlife.

Now let's look at Jim in the new era *after* the gods. This Jim also has an average job, friends, and a family. Jim is not even aware of gods, as that was a belief of an era long past. Jim understands where he comes from, and he marvels and takes pride in the wonderful process of evolution that resulted in the remarkably diverse abundance of life on Earth. Jim has a decent understanding of evolution and the world around him. He also knows how the solar system and the Earth were formed, and finds the idea fascinating and logical. He enjoys explaining it to his kids. Jim is also appreciative of life and the beauty of the world and universe, and he feels the vibrancy of it all around him.

Jim has a set of moral values that he internalized years ago, during his childhood and early adulthood. These moral values help Jim find a place in the community he lives in, and also in his interaction with other individuals and his family. Jim knows that one day he will die, and understands the biological process involved. He does not have to worry about the afterlife. He believes that if there's an afterlife, it will be for everyone. He finds meaning in his present life, lives it to the fullest, and gives back to the world he lives in. He knows that life presents a person with many opportunities, and that it's up to him to make full use of this reality.

As we find a new framework and meaning of life, our society and culture will begin to mirror the second Jim's. Most advanced countries have already segregated religion from government, and have structures in place to use reason and fact to make decisions—e.g. legal systems and constitutional courts. As the ancient religions are displaced, countries will start adopting a stance of reason and human secularity rather than the current bias towards a god. The remaining religions will find themselves existing within an administrative system of reason, rationality and justice—directly the opposite of today's prevailing conditions, in which reason and science must try to coexist under the umbrella of religious dogma and irrational ideology.

The new awakening of reason and rationality will set the governance framework of each country, including the way it interacts with the world. Again, this is not a passive philosophy. These countries will act aggressively, if required, to defend themselves against aggression, including that generated by unquestioned dogma, unfounded superstition, beliefs calling for the obliteration of others, hatred, and other destructive philosophies—many of which have a theological basis, sadly.

We can envisage that such a country would have an impartial and objective legal body to look at matters without interference, bias, or emotions. Reason and facts would be used in the decision-making process. A system to segregate the powers of the state and ensure checks and balances would be in place. As George Smith remarked in his 1979 book *Atheism: The Case Against God*, one requirement of a civilized society is a legal system to protect the individual from the aggressive activities of those around him.

CHAPTER 5

The Last 100 Years of Religion

I can see a future where the fog of religion is lifting. I can see a new world where religion no longer exists. I can see the human race finally grasping its true origins, and using its intellect to further its understanding, purpose, and reason within this wide and wonderful Universe.

A New Era Without Gods

We human beings are becoming more knowledgeable and conscious about our world. As far as we know, no other species on Earth has ever reached the same level of development. This immense universe, governed by the laws of physics that also ultimately produced life and fine-tuned it via the mechanism of evolution, now contains a species, which observes, documents, and understands it. This species has become acutely conscious of the universe, and also of itself. This species has also become painfully aware of the individual's short lifetime within the grand panorama of our vast universe. A typical human being can live for 80-100 years at most, with its only possible legacies the passing on of its DNA to its offspring, possibly a few pieces of art and literature, and any cultural changes brought about within the species itself (i.e. raising a child a certain way, shaping political thought, or inventing something).

Having knowledge and consciousness gives our species immense power, but also pain. We can now consciously change the universe, or manipulate life itself by restructuring genomes. But despite our progress, we are still a product of evolution, with fallible brains and belief structures. We're prone to superstition; at times, our emotional, cultural, or religious convictions keep us from making the right decisions. Our species still grapples to understand its place in the universe, and also the universe itself. Being self-aware is no easy task.

If we destroy ourselves—and now we can, with a relatively little effort—the universe will keep moving forward as before. Despite what we'd like to believe, it doesn't care about us humans. If there is life left, that life will continue to follow its evolutionary path, and some distant day a new species may lift itself into an epoch of conscious thought.

Biological Aging and the Death of the Individual

Unless you happen to be a member of the jellyfish species *Turritopsis nutricula*, which continuously replaces its cells with healthy ones and lives until killed by accident or predation, your life will have a finite span.

When a human egg and sperm join, each containing 23 chromosomes to create a total of 46, a new individual is created with a unique genetic code resulting from the fusion of the mother's and father's genes. This same process repeats itself in different forms all over the natural world—from the sea coral that release sperm and eggs in a milky cloud to form new life, to the bee that takes pollen from one flower to the next. It's all part of an evolutionary process with origins rooted billions of years ago. But even as it produces new life, this process ultimately produces death, when all biological functions terminate.

Almost all life undergoes biological aging. Aging rates differ from species to species. The bristlecone pine tree can live up to 5,000 years, the common fruit fly up to 30 days. We *Homo sapiens* specimens can expect about 85 years, more or less. Once physical maturity has been reached, biological aging immediately begins. We still don't know the exact mechanisms involved in aging, for there are many factors that contribute to it. In humans, one major factor is the shortening of telomeres, or the end pieces of chromosomes. They shorten by 50-200 base pairs every time the cell divides. Over time, the telomeres become so eroded that they lose their ability to protect the chromosome, so that cell quality declines with each repetition. This is called cell senescence.

Other factors involved in aging include damage to the DNA from background radiation, free radicals, and viral infection, as well as dividing errors. All lead to further loss of healthy proteins and cells. There is now also evidence that our cells contain genes that actually cause aging—in other words, Death is encoded in our genome. We are genetically programmed to age.

The accumulation of damage over a lifetime leads to a declining ability to deal with environmental stress. The heart that used to be strong and healthy is no longer new. Its impaired ability, coupled with higher blood pressure, may eventually cause it to fail. When that happens, the biological organism relying on the provisioning of oxygen to its cells breaks down and terminates. Similarly, the immune system of a very old person may be overwhelmed by the invasion of a foreign virus or bacterium, becoming defenseless to the intruder.

In addition to aging, other biological changes can kill us. Cancer, the uncontrollable growth of malicious cells, can invade and displace healthy tissue. The human body can also cease to function due to extensive trauma to life-sustaining functions—e.g., the blade of a knife entering a major artery.

Aging and death are part of the evolutionary mechanism. Once we have produced offspring and passed on our genes, there is little more use for us in the great evolutionary process.

Figure 13: The natural process of biological aging in one human being

A species that dies young but leaves plenty of offspring will have greater fitness to survive and evolve. There is no evolutionary advantage to staying young (the previous generation needs to make way for the new generation with its new genes), and evolution does not benefit in selecting those genes which may make us live longer. Up to now, death has been a prerequisite for a species to evolve.

As our species evolved, we became increasingly aware of ourselves and the world around us. We become conscious—and for that, we had to pay a price. We came to understand the concept of personal death and the inevitability of it. Despite all we have done—the love found and nurtured, attachments made, our value to ourselves and others—it will all pass. Each of us knows, if we bother to think about it, that one day we will cease to exist. One's body will become part of the biogeochemical cycle again, broken down again into its chemical components or becoming part of the food chain.

The psychological impact of such a realization may have a profound impact on the individual, creating an underlying anxiety, since death can strike at any time. One might step in front of an oncoming car, or a terminal illness might strike; however it happens, it *will* happen. We can take precautions and go for annual health checkups to increase our chances of survival, but none of us can guarantee that we will live another year.

From the very beginning of self awareness, death has caused humans to invent all kinds of rituals and cultural habits to cope with it; so to a large degree, our development of ritual and religion took place in direct relationship to our awareness and consciousness of our own deaths, a development that culminated in today's gods and religions. These religions offer, on the strength of a particular god, assurance of an afterlife—an escape from the inevitability of death.

The wish for an eternal carefree life spent with loved ones is, in fact, the primary enticement used by almost every religion to maintain control of its followers. This fear of death makes many of us blatantly ignore the evidence we have compiled opposing the ideologies of most religions. But by now the evidence has become overwhelming, and we are awakened to religion's pious deceptions as our advances in science and knowledge continue. The ancient religions and their gods are increasingly under attack. The scriptures supporting them have been exposed as the compilations of ancient authors, many not directly associated with the prophets and messiahs they claim to report the words of, having been cherry-picked, adapted, and edited by those who came after to better fit their conceptions of a holy text.

On the one hand, the gods provide the comfort of providing an escape from death. On the other, our intellect and knowledge tells us that religions and their gods are irrational—and none of these gods *ever* shows his presence or proves his existence. However, religions explain away that as a test of faith. But we all know the truth, deep inside. Death is *not* a premeditated or planned activity on the part of a supernatural being. It is simply one of the attributes of biological life.

If we can free ourselves from the stranglehold of religion, and the concept that the afterworld (if it exists) is reserved only for believers, then with the help of our scientific knowledge we can transform ourselves into modern beings who truly understand ourselves and the world around us. I have no doubt that in doing so, we will accelerate our understanding of ourselves and the universe, enabling us to lead better lives, furthering the evolution of ourselves, life in general, and the universe as a whole.

Purpose and Meaning without Gods

One of the most common questions asked by the religious is how the non-religious find purpose in life. After all, most religious teachings hold that the entire purpose of life is to gain acceptance and mercy from a god. Without this belief, they argue, we will fall into despair and depression. Life will become so meaningless that we will be without direction, which will cause us to give up hope, destroying others along with ourselves. Why does life matter—and how can it have a purpose—if we're little more than the byproducts of a chance chemical bond that led to a special molecule that somehow stumbled upon a mechanism of self-replication, and all that followed? There is no afterlife, no one to greet and resurrect us in the outer darkness.

We all ask these questions of ourselves and the world:

- Why are we here?
- Why does the universe exists?
- What is life all about?
- What is the meaning of it all?

Surely, our purpose is *not* just that of serving a god, and begging for his benevolence. Yet billions of people have made this the central belief of their lives. For most, during the last few years before death, much time is spent contemplating one's life, weighing one's actions and wondering whether one has done enough and was obedient enough to find a place in the afterlife. In Judaism, Christianity, and Islam, the central dogma is to find mercy by showing one's belief in God or Allah. Unbelievers will be banished to everlasting agony by their "loving" God, and suffer for eternity. This God, we are told, wants to see us worship and love him—though He has never revealed himself to us. That this seems rather arrogant and narcissistic is ignored. But in any case it is all a delusion—the god is manmade, with feet of clay. There *is* no one to punish us. So here's the truly Good News: there is no Hell. If there's afterlife, it will be open to all.

But the religious wail, "If we don't have gods, then what is the purpose of life? Can we find purpose without our gods?"

However the absence of a god does *not* mean that life has no purpose, or that our existence is meaningless or hopeless. As a matter of fact, there is so much more purpose in life than those limited, insubstantial reasons provided by pseudo-religions. Adam Lee (Lee) summarized it well:

"In fact, my life is overflowing with purpose. It is full of meaning. To me, atheism is a life of wonder. I find it in the simple company of friends and the deeper and more profound company of someone I love. I find it in watching the sun rise at dawn. I find it in walking through a forest in autumn and marveling at the vibrancy of color and the play of sunlight on leaves, walking through the same forest in summer, observing photosynthesis and the interlocking and vibrant web of life produced by millions of years of evolution, returning to that forest in winter to see the fractal patterns of branches and frost and the turbulence of my breath steaming in the air. I find it in watching the flight of birds. I find it in watching clouds at day and considering how atmospheric scatter of sunlight makes the sky appear blue, or watching stars at night and letting my imagination drift through the incomparable vastness and grandeur of the cosmos, wondering whether there is any other intelligent life out there that might at that moment be wondering the same thing. I find it in reflecting on deep truths of my own existence, picturing my own thoughts as electrochemical flashes in a network of neurons and synapses, my own body as proteins built up by self-replicating double helixes, shearing and recombining, mutating and propagating themselves through deep time, my own structure as composed of glittering bits of matter, the whirl of electrons around the atomic nuclei, tiny immutable particles both as old as the universe and as ephemeral as nothingness, all self-assembling over multiple levels of complexity into a thinking, conscious mind that can reflect on its own existence. I find it in contemplating the future and wondering what will come next. There is much to enjoy in this world, and none of it is made any less valid or desirable by not believing in God. Instead, it only increases my wonder that we exist, that we live and think, that we have come this far by ourselves. There is much for us to love, much for us to value, and very much still for us to learn. This is not nihilism, and there is no reason for it to be. On the contrary, atheism is nothing less than a resounding affirmation of life. "

Knowing more about our world makes a person more appreciative of seeing it. Let's say a person is looking out over the Grand Canyon. The uninformed believer will see this as the creation of God and admire its beauty as proof of the greatness of God. A non-believer will also be filled with awe and admiration, in wonder at the millions of years it took to slowly carve the canyon by erosion. He wonders how it must have looked in the past, and what our ancient forefathers thought as they peered out at it. Similarly, though a believer might be awed by the majesty and wonder of a distant mountain range as a demonstration of God's power, the rationalist's awe will be at the incredible geological processes involved, and the explainable workings of the tectonic plates that pushed up the mountain range. Let's take a look at the different meanings of life espoused by various religions, and contrast them with the non-religious viewpoint:

- **Judaism**: to serve God, and prepare for the world to come.
- **Christianity**: to find salvation by the grace of God through Jesus Christ, in order to attain the afterlife.
- **Islam**: to serve Allah and his teachings in order to attain the afterlife.
- **Hinduism**: there are four stages of the meaning of life. In the last, we reach Moksha, liberation from the material world.
- **Buddhism**: to detach oneself from the cravings and suffering of the world to reach Nirvana.
- **Secular humanism**: finds individual purpose and common good for all people.
- **Non-belief**: finds solace in the wonders of the world, cosmos, and our evolutionary origins. Each person determines their own

purpose in life, and aspires to the further development of knowledge, life, and the world.

We have a responsibility to continue, to further ourselves and our understanding of the universe, to chart and shape our future and that of life in the universe. As far as we know, only the human race exists to further this purpose; and even if we are not alone in the cosmos, in one sense or another we owe it to ourselves and our posterity to find some deeper understanding of ourselves and the world around us. We must be especially diligent in guarding against those who want to drag us back to a world of superstition and unfounded ideology.

As a result of our evolutionary origins, we are all different, sprinkled with a variety of talents, feelings and emotions as a result of the interaction of our inherited genes and the external environment. We all take different paths in our lives, with the individual experiences and perceptions that result. Our different make-ups make each of us perceive and handle life differently. Some of us are rich, some are poor. Some of us are economically average but live rich lives; some of us die unhappy and resentful.

It is up to each of us, individually, to find inner peace and a place in the world. The world abounds with opportunities to sustain ourselves emotionally, and to find our niches within this vast and wonderful cosmos. The ways can be complex or simple. One can walk along an empty beach, gaze up at night at a star-filled sky, spend time in a garden or mountains, or sit on the curb the hour before the city gets busy. There is so much that we can and should do.

And while the above may satisfy our emotional needs, the next section puts into place a new framework to help us better understand ourselves and the world.

Seeing the World Through New Eyes

As we leave our ancient religions and beliefs behind us, we will perceive and interpret the world differently. Instead of viewing the world through the tainted lenses of religion, we will see and perceive it based on our knowledge and understanding of the universe and ourselves.

The "I" will know where our species came from, and take pride in its development and knowledge. The "I" will know how the Earth was really created, and realize that the human species is the result of a long evolutionary chain of life originating in a primordial ocean. This knowledge is curiously liberating, for it provides the "I" with a feeling of belonging, and allows individuals to increase their comprehension of life and the universe at large.

As the "I" gazes up to the stars at night, it will feel the immenseness of the cosmos. The "I" will develop a better, healthier understanding of the micro-world around him/her, those microscopic particles and miniscule energies that comprise the macro-world. The "I" will come to appreciate its significance in this world as something more than just a small creature created expressly to idolize a god. The "I" will endeavor to understand this world better, whether in the emotional sense or in the scientific sense that governs our world. The "I" will know that within itself is the DNA that serves as the blueprint of life.

As the "I" looks around, it will see other humans, and the "I" will better understand the different human traits. The "I" will know about his or her own psychological make-up, and understand why he or she behaves in a certain way. The "I" will be strong in advocating reason and the quest for knowledge, and aspire to the further development of knowledge, life, and the world.

The "I" will find meaning and love in the world to satisfy his/her emotional needs, and will aid in building successful and emotionally satisfying communities.

Support for Our Species as Social Animals

One must recognize that the existing religious institutions have been very successful in building support structures for their adherents. Even for those for whom no hope exists—where grinding poverty has reduced them to beggars, or for those in crisis—the religious establishment provides support. The downtrodden, the desolate, the lonely, and the struggling can turn to their religious establishment for love and acceptance—a place where the individual (ideally) will not be judged by his or her achievements or material wealth, but where this person is taken in as an individual or soul that is equal and deserves love and acceptance. One cannot ignore the social needs of our species.

Religions provide assistance, in environments where the time and resources of other believers are used to support and sustain the unfortunate. (Previously, the tribe handled this, but these support structures disappeared with the advent of the Industrial Revolution). A mosque, church, or monastery may include a group of committed people who, without compensation, provide love, food, and attention to those in need. Many children in poverty and from abusive families have found haven and support foundations within a religious establishment.

So who will serve these purposes as we move beyond our religious era? Who will provide the same kinds of support structures, in which unselfish dedication and care can be given to those in need? How will we protect these support structures from those grasping for power and recognition? In this case, the incentive of a reward in the afterlife does not exist. Any assistance must be provided as a duty and contribution to life, our species, and a better future for all—an unselfish duty that moves us forward as we leave our ancient religions behind.

In 1943, Abraham Maslow published a paper outlining what motivates and satisfies human needs. The basis for his study was a sample of individuals that he observed to determine their motivations, requirements, and levels of happiness. Although Maslow's model has since been refined, it still serves as a basic model for understanding what drives us.

Maslow identified five basic levels. In the first, a human has basic needs, namely breathing, food, and water. A hungry man is so preoccupied with survival that his whole being and actions are directed toward it. Love, beauty, politics, and other needs become non-essential or pushed aside; survival is foremost. Religious establishments provide food, water, and shelter to those in need; though today, many governmental entities also provide social support, which diminishes the need for religious institutions to provide it.

Once this level is satisfied, the next need will arise: to be safe, including financial security, health, and well-being. Religion starts playing a role in this level, as belonging provides a safe haven if one is threatened. This is especially important in dangerous neighborhoods, where gangs or abusive parents may be a threat to the child, and the child finds safety in the church or support groups.

In the third level, love and belonging are required. We all have a need to be loved and accepted, and to have intimate relationships or friends. A religious group can provide these needs, or otherwise create the opportunities to fulfill them: e.g., arranging a gathering, matchmaking, and participating in religious activities. The lonely or unloved person may find acceptance or love in a religious institution, as these are values that most religions uphold.

In Maslow's fourth level, we have a need to be respected, with a desire to be valued and recognized by others. Again, a religious institution may provide these.

In the fifth level there is a need for self-actualization. Maslow describes this as a situation in which we have a desire to fulfill our potential, to sense our purpose in life, and also to serve others and life itself. We can break free from our material desires, overcoming our human emotions of jealously and hate. We move beyond daily struggle to a new level. Buddhism has been very much focused on this level, driving self-actualization by requiring its adherents to give love and compassion to those around them.

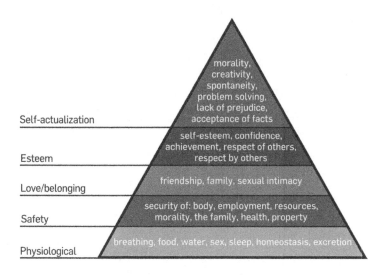

Figure 14: Maslow's hierarchy of human needs

As we move away from our ancient religions and gods, we will have to build the same support structures and satisfy our human needs as shown above. After all, aren't we social animals? Religions have been shaped over the ages to meet our emotional needs, but we need to move beyond these ancient, outdated social structures to new ones that incorporate our new understanding of the world and cosmos, while providing the love and support human beings need.

Raising Our Children

As we move deeper into our new, rational world, our children will be raised in a new era, where existing knowledge and science are used to instruct them instead of religion. Rather than explaining and entertaining irrational universes ruled over by cruel gods of punishment, we will endeavor to explain to our children the wonders of the universe, Earth, and life in general. We will explain their roles in the great scheme, and the gift that this life truly is—without forcing them to spend their lives constantly thanking a false creator.

We will teach the new generations how to find themselves in this world, how to become healthy adults, and how to remain resilient in the face of challenges and the pain of life. We will also endeavor to be good parents with good parenting skills, and to set boundaries for unacceptable behavior. There are no magic formulas for child-rearing; each child will need his or her own approach. There are, however, a few universals to good parenting that every parent would do well to heed:

1. Set an example for your children in your own behavior, and how you interact with the world and others.
2. Love your children, and strike the balance between being a parent and a friend.
3. Be involved in your child's life.
4. Adapt your parenting to fit the child. Each child has his or her own personality.
5. Establish and enforce rules. A child without boundaries will learn the wrong habits, and may turn out to be quite unpleasant.
6. Assist and encourage your child's independence.
7. Be consistent in your parenting, and present a united front and approach with your spouse.
8. Avoid harsh discipline. Be firm, but not degrading and humiliating.
9. Talk to your child, explaining your rules and decisions.
10. Treat your child with respect.

The above is not intended to be complete, but only to serve as a starting point for parents. The days when children are raised to be obedient and submissive to a god, with a fear of that god's punishment if they stray, are on their way out the door—and good riddance. Teaching a child a religion does not make the child a better person; guiding and teaching him or her with respect, love, firmness, and fairness does.

The world is filled of children who have gone astray despite strict religious upbringings, for the simple reason that the above parenting skills were absent from their lives. They never had the opportunity to be raised with affection, love, and respect. Of course, the world is also full of kids who had non-religious parents who never gave them love and attention either. But then again, there are plenty who were raised with caring and love, such that they were able to give back caring and love. And then there are those who, with all the odds against them, rose above their poor upbringings to be full of love and caring nonetheless.

The message is simple: an environment of care, love, and attention is the ultimate factor in raising a good kid, not his god or religion.

Living in a World after Religion

The human race is on the cusp of a major change in the way it thinks and perceives the world. The knowledge we have acquired in the past 100 years alone has allowed us to more fully understand our physical and emotional worlds. Our decrepit religions no longer provide the answers we need, despite ardent believers and untiring efforts to convert others to their irrational and outdated beliefs. The universe is opening to us—and soon some of our race may reside beyond the Earth.

The time has come for a radical change. We must abolish our ancient religions and move into a new era of knowledge and understanding. There is no longer the prerequisite of a specific belief to find an afterlife. If there *is* an afterlife, it is, logically, open to all of us. If our current gods refuse to agree to this monumental change in the world, then it is time for them to reveal themselves and tell us so.

The absence of the gods can be seen as their acceptance of this new era—or more realistically, as proof that they never existed in the first place.

As we move forward into this new era, there will be a painful transition period, during which the religious establishments will struggle to retain their beliefs and gods, motivated by an unfounded fear of these gods and a fear of not achieving the afterlife. No doubt there will also be backlashes as the privileged hierarchies within those religious structures refuse to relinquish their earthly power. The religious machinery will launch a smear campaign, labeling unbelievers as evil or subhuman, the onslaught of the Devil against the good and righteous. Indeed, we can see this happening already on a daily basis.

But the tide is turning, and as this new movement starts taking shape, we need to put our backs into the effort of building an image and reputation for ourselves. This will form our defense against un-founded allegations, while we persistently challenge their irrational beliefs. In our transformation from god/myth religions to reason and science, we will strive to:

1. Sustain our human morals as best described by humanity.
2. Take care of the unfortunate and the poor.
3. Endeavor to set an example of fairness, honesty, and goodness.
4. Be factual, and open-minded to new facts.
5. Champion knowledge as gained by observation, experimentation, and rational analysis—the scientific method.
6. Continue our relentless search to understand the world and the cosmos.
7. Continue sustaining and aiding life in the universe, wherever we find it.
8. Enrich our own lives, the lives of those around us, and the world in general.

In the new world the individual will:

1. Perceive the origins of the world and life as explained by science.
2. Understand the psychological make-up of humankind.
3. Find inner peace, contentment, and fulfillment in life and the world.
4. Live his/her life fully, with a sense of purpose.
5. Overcome the challenges in life, even in the face of the inevitability and finality of death.
6. Perform social work and unselfish work at times for those in need.
7. See death as an attribute of biological life, which we may well overcome in the future.
8. Find consolation and peace in the knowledge of his/her own death.
9. Be impartial to an afterlife; if it is there, it is open to all.
10. Support science and the advancement of life and human life in the universe.

The Time Has Come

As I stand on the endless beach, and the solitude of the blue skies and vast ocean fill my soul, I feel the wind and the warmth of the sun on my skin, and revel in the sounds of nature. I feel the ancient Earth and the universe around me. I am conscious of my body and the DNA and other biochemical structures that have evolved to make me conscious and self-aware. I feel the life around me, which has evolved over the past few billion years. I dream of a world where the last church bells will sound, and the prayer call of the mosques will fall silent; where the Hindu gods will be forgotten, and the final religions fade away. I dream of a new era, where we human beings will move beyond our ancient beliefs, myths, and religions. I dream of a world where reason, science, and justice will prevail for each and every one of us.

And as I hear the seagulls shriek above me, I scoop up a handful of seawater and wash my face. The cruelty and blood of our religions rinses away, and the new day dawns.

A world without religion.

A world where our children will no longer know our ancient gods.

The time has come for our children to be atheists.

References

Aggett, S., 2012. *The evolution of the world's religions from beginning to present.* [Online] . Available at: http://www.religionstree.com. [Accessed 6 August 2012].

Boyce, M., 2001. *Zoroastrians: Their Religious Beliefs and Practices.* 2 ed. s.l.: Routledge.

Burr, G. L., 1896. *The Witch Persecutions from translations and reprints from the original sources of European History. VOL. III. No. 4..* s.l.: s.n.

Charlesworth, J. H., 2008. *Resurrection: The Origin and Future of a Biblical Doctrine.* s.l.: T&T Clark.

Christian Smith, R. F., 2002. *Religion and the Life Attitudes and Self-Images of American Adolescents,* University of North Carolina: National Study of Youth and Religion.

Church of England, n.d. *The Church of England.* [Online]. Available at: http://www.churchofengland.org/education/church-schools-academies.aspx [Accessed 2 1 2012].

Coles, R., 1991. *The Spiritual Life of Children.* 1 ed. s.l.: Houghton Mifflin Harcourt.

Faris, N. A., 1952. *The Book of Idols, being a translation from the Arabic of the Kitab Al-Asnam by Hisham Ibn-Al-Kalbi.* s.l.: Princeton University Press.

Fox, J., 2008. *A World Survey of Religion and the State.* New York: Cambridge University Press.

231

Griffith, Ralph T.H., n.d. *Internet Sacred Text Archive.* [Online] Available at: http://www.sacred-texts.com/hin/rigveda/index.htm [Accessed 6 September 2012].

Humanism, C. f. S., n.d. *What Is Secular Humanism?* [Online] Available at: http://www.secularhumanism.org/index.php?page=what&section=main [Accessed 14 September 2012].

Hume, R. E., 1921. *The Thirteen Principal Upanishads: Translated from the Sanskrit with an Outline of the Philosophy of the Upanishads.* s.l.: Oxford University Press.

Josephus, F., 1737. *The Works of Flavius Josephus, translated by William Whiston.* s.l.: s.n.

Kohlberg, L., 1976. Moral stages and moralization: The cognitive-developmental approach. In: T. E. Lickona, ed. *Moral Development and Behavior: Theory, Research and Social Issues.* New York: Holt, Rinehart & Winston , pp. 31-53.

Lee. A., 2013. *Life of Wonder, viewed August 2013.* [Online]. Available at: http://www.patheos.com/blogs/daylightatheism/essays/life-of-wonder [Accessed 9 August 2013].

Marcus J. F. K., 2004. The coevolution of ritual and society: new 14C dates from ancient Mexico. *Proc Natl Acad Sci U S A,* 101(52): 18257-61.

Nielsen, M. E., n.d. *Religion and Happiness, viewed January 2012.* [Online]. Available at: http://www.psywww.com/psyrelig/happy.htm [Accessed 10 January 2012].

Outram, D., 2005. *The Enlightenment: New Approaches to European History.* s.l.: Cambridge University Press.

Rank, O., 1909. *Der Mythus von der Geburt des Helden.* Wien-Leipzig: Franz Deuticke.

Shahar Arzy, M. I. T. L. O. B., 2005. Why have revelations occurred on mountains? Linking mystical experiences and cognitive neuroscience. *Medical Hypotheses,* 65: 841–845.

Smith, G. H., 1979. In: *Atheism: The Case Against God.* s.l.: Nash, p. 83. Wikipedia, n.d.

Würzburg witch trial. [Online]. Available at: http://en.wikipedia.org/wiki/W%C3%BCrzburg_witch_trial [Accessed February 1, 2012].

Made in the USA
Las Vegas, NV
31 January 2023

66574756R00134